A Walk in the Sunshine

The Inspirational Writings
of
Helene Clare Kuoni

A Walk in the Sunshine: Inspirational Writings of Helene Clare Kuoni

Copyright © 2019 Helene C. Kuoni

ISBN 978-0-578-48793-9 (Paperback)
ISBN 2-370000-686626 (Hardbound)

Author: Helene C. Kuoni
Photography: Helene C. Kuoni
Production: John P. Kuoni

All rights reserved. No part of this publication may be reproduced or transmitted in any form or by any means without the written permission of the publisher, except by a reviewer who may quote brief passages for a review.

Scripture quotations marked (NIV) are taken from the *Holy Bible, New International Version.* Copyright © 1973, 1978, 1984 International Bible Society. Used by permission of Zondervan Bible Publishers.

Scripture quotations marked (GW) are taken from *GOD's WORD® Translation.* Copyright © 1995 God's Word to the Nations. Used by permission.

Scripture quotations marked (NLT) are taken from the *Holy Bible,* New Living Translation. Copyright © 1996, 2004, 2007 Tindale House Foundation. Used by permission of Tyndale House Publishers, Inc., Carol Stream, Illinois 60188. All rights reserved.

Scripture quotations marked (KJV) are from the *King James Version of the Bible*.

Cover: Granite fountain (1871) of City Hall Park, New York, NY.

Printing: September 24, 2020

List of Books by Author

Helene
  A Walk in the Sunshine: The Inspirational Writings of Helene Clare Kuoni
  The Hollwegs Choir Journal (limited edition)

John and Helene
  Her Pen for His Glory: The 1860s Verse of Isabella Stiles (sic, Stites) Mead
  The Diaries of Genevieve Cole (limited edition)

John
  The Diaries of Genevieve Cole, 1911, 1913-1917
  The Education of Genevieve Cole, Born 1894 (limited edition)
  The Troller Photo Album (limited edition)

Table of Contents

In Appreciation ix
Preface xi
Solid Ground of God's Word 1
    Forwarding Mail 3
    Touchdown! 5
    Whose Leaf Does Not Wither 7
    Eve Misquoted 9
    Read Your Bible 10
    First Class Mail 10
Fair Days of Fellowship and Church 11
    What's Really Broken? 13
    The Mantle Passed 15
    Condemned 17
    Worship Styles 19
    Old-Fashioned Coffee Time 20
    The Belfry 22
    Remember Me 23
    Dorothy's All-Time Favorite Carol 24
Sunrise of New Beginnings 29
    Out of Kilter 31
    Loss and Gain 33
    Green, but Not Growing 34
    The Key to Undoing 35
Sun, Moon, and Stars – God's Faithfulness in Nature 37
    Remain True 38

    Trustworthy Timbers 38
    Beauty Secrets 39
    Hold Fast to Your Faith 40
    Faithful in One Concern 42
    Fickle? Me? 43
    Daily Steps 44
    Wise Investments 45
    Keeping the Faith 46

Fog of Fear and Indecision 53
    Me – At Age Three 54
    The Timeless Message of Love 55
    Courage in C Major 56

Refreshing Times of Friendship 59
    Friendship Helps 61
    Bragging Rights 63
    True Friends 64
    A Heart Made Fit for Friendship 65
    Christmas 2008 66

Billowing Clouds of Witness 73
    Distinguished 74
    Tracks in the Snow 77
    Show or Tell 78
    To the Jungles! 79
    A City on a Hill 80
    Anna and Ina 81
    Multiplying the Light 82

Waterfalls of God's Love 83

Stereotypes 84
The Unveiling 85
See for Yourself 87
To Curry Favor 88
No Angels, Please 91
Unclassified 92
The Best Heart-Shaped Greeting in the World 93

Morningstar, Direction of the Family 95
My Dad's Christmas 96
Mom 98
Dad 100
Drummer Dad 103
Clothed in Her Love 107
Saturday Morning Eggy-Peggy 109

Dawn of the Holy Spirit 111
Recognizing Jesus 112
Enlightened 113
The Comforter 114
Dorcas-Like 115
The Houseguest Who Never Leaves 115
The Manager 117
Epiphany 118
Bread of Life 120

Orbits of Kingdom Work 123
Lordship of Jesus 124
Limitations 124
Workers Who Please God 125

Time Management	127
Formula for Good Results	128
Get Moving!	129
Encouragement for Our Troops	129
Marilyn's Shoe Bag	130
Full Employment	131
Good Gossip	132
Power Lunch	134
Fair Dealings	135
Goodness	136

Threatening Storm Clouds of Difficulty ... 139

The Puffback	140
The Single Funniest Event in Our Marriage	144
A Lesson from Arithmetic	145
God's Family	145

Flames of Prayer ... 147

"Take It to the Lord in Prayer"	148
Forward March!	148
Battle of the Buns	149
Good Counsel	151
A Place of Prayer	152
Lugar para la oración	153
When Timing was Everything	154

God's Promises and Power in Creation ... 157

The Sky-High Promise	158
God's Secret Work	161
I'm Listening	162

The Lover's Promise	163
Mightier than Creation	165
"Let All Mortal Flesh Keep Silence"	166
Uphill Battles and Bountiful Blessings	168

Sunset Rest 173

Relax	175
Neglected Miracle	177
The Unopened Gift	178
Memories	179
Mary at Prayer	180
Collection of Treasures	182

Harvest of Salvation 183

In Need of a Good Scrubbing	185
The Lamb's Book of Life	187
Light for the Lost	188
Be an Agent of Change	189

Storms of Temptation 191

Preparing for Snakes	192
Danger!	193
Train Ride	193

Nighttime of Trust and Peace 195

Don't Borrow Trouble	197
No Matter Where	199
Deep Waters	201
Beauty in the Darkest Sky	203
Sure Steps	204
Handling Anger	205

    Sometimes It's Best Not to Listen! 206
    Relinquishing My Will 208

Clear Skies of Thankfulness 211
    Daily Guideposts Reader's Room: A Helping Hand 212
    Baby's First Word 213

Trails to Travel 215
    Traveling Light 216
    Gotland – Top and Center 217
    Dalarna First 220
    Cruising the Göta Canal 223
    NORDLEK '85 with Swedish Folk Dancers 226

Dewdrops of Wisdom 229
    Dorothy 230
    Growing Up 232
    Truth Telling 233
    Picture It! 234
    Godly Destination 235
    Whose Way? 237
    A Royal Education 238
    Fighting 239
    Setting Goals 239
    Turn Off that Boombox 239
    My Life Changed the Day I Got Stuck in the Elevator 240

Gardens of Grace 243
    Serving with a Smile 244
    Crocuses and Grace 245
    Whom will You Serve? 246

    Lighten Up!.. 248
    Miss Lungen's Legacy 250

Moonglow of Childhood Memories................................ 253
    My Two.. 258
    Thanksgiving Day Parade 259
    Saint Patrick's Day Parade... 262

The Wellspring of Words... 267
    News! News! A Birth! 268
    Get to the Point 269
    Jump Right In.. 270
    Nobody's Perfect 271
    Genevieve's Journal... 272
    Yet, Not Yet, and You Bet! 274

About the Author... 278

References 281

In Appreciation

The Lord has placed wonderful mentors in my life. A few, listed here in historical sequence, especially influenced my writing efforts.

Mom* – taught me that a sentence consists of subject and predicate; and that I should end my sentences with a period every so often. Promised I'd have lots to share after I'd "lived a bit." Always kind and nurturing.

Dad* – demonstrated strong work ethic and always strove for excellence. Strong, yet sentimental.

My sisters **Thyra, Dorothy*** and **Marilyn** – always there for me.

Thyra – helped me find a teaching position (English as a Second Language) at P.S. 17, Queens, NY. Provided support as I handled public relations over 10 years of The Hollwegs Choir. Supplied lots of statistics for *The Hollwegs Choir Journal.*

Dorothy* – surprised me with a small camera for my purse and said I should take notes and pictures wherever I went. She (employed by Texaco) introduced me (employed by Mobil Oil) to the Association of Desk & Derrick Clubs. Together we won awards for our work as co-editors of the D&D New York Club's bi-monthly publication.

Marilyn – always willingly offers feedback and proof-reading services. She, together with Thyra and Dorothy, gave support as I handled public relations over 10 years of The Hollwegs Choir. Marilyn shared ideas, photos, and contributed a chapter to *The Hollwegs Choir Journal.*

Karen Olsen Coy, poet and lifelong friend – who often reminds me to "Keep writing!" Introduced me to *Penned from the Heart* and other Christian markets. Always makes me laugh.

Mrs. Helen Olsen,* Karen's mom - who kept an album of clippings, favorite pieces that spoke to her heart. Showed me that a word fitly "spoken" is treasured, re-read and enjoyed many times. Often encouraged me in my writing efforts.

William Dehnert,* FDNY Band member (Brass) and violin teacher – who told me "Nothing worthwhile is accomplished easily."

Reverend Dr. Bernard Brunsting,* Greenville Community Reformed Church, Scarsdale, NY – who once preached a sermon, explaining *how* he wrote and preached a sermon. Never forgot the advice he unwittingly shared with me, a budding writer taking notes that Sunday.

Reverend Jack Traugott,* a campus chaplain (Hunter College), and Pastor at Emanuel Lutheran Church, Pleasantville, NY – for his one-word counsel: "Yet."

Reverend William Gillies Kalaidjian,* NYPD Senior Protestant Chaplain for 42 years and Pastor at Bedford Park Congregational Church, Bronx, NY – who trusted me to begin writing his life's story.

Frances Gregory Pasch, poet, devotion writer, gracious host of long-running critique group – for welcoming me into a fellowship of fine writers. We always rely on Fran to provide great advice! Good friend.

Kathleen Hayes, Editor - who gave me the opportunity to work for her at Judson Press (*The Secret Place*) and became a friend.

Liberty Corner Presbyterian Church, NJ – introduced me to member-written Advent devotional guides. I led this effort for 11 years.

Union Evangelical Lutheran Church, Schnecksville, PA – for embracing the devotional guide idea. I led this effort for five years.

"My" John – It is impossible to list here all that he does and all that he means. (Besides, he asked me not to.) Suffice it to say, I *am* blessed!

All the above - precious brothers and sisters in Christ, for whom I thank and praise God!   - HCK

*Resting from their labors, in our Heavenly Father's keeping.

Preface

When I was quite young I told my mom I wished to become a writer. She wisely counselled that I first needed to grow up and "live a bit." Then I'd have experiences to write about.

As I look back, that's exactly how my writing career evolved. Though never employed as a full-time writer, my various work assignments, church activities, clubs and professional associations offered me ample opportunity to hone my communication skills. I also enjoyed studying Scripture through the years. Oh how I've always loved to delve into the riches of God's Word!

So I "lived a bit," and found I'd amassed lots of personal experiences to write about. Early retirement afforded me time to participate in a Christian writers' critique group. Soon I began to submit my work to publishers of devotional material.

At first I felt sheepish opening my heart to public scrutiny. I feared I'd reveal too many of my shortcomings and foibles. Soon I discovered that the personal weaknesses I shared did not shock any readers. Instead, readers could relate! We are all human and my opening up often helped others face their own issues.

I also discovered some surprises as I wrote. Problem areas surfaced to reveal where I needed to do better in my life. It's how I've dealt with worry and fear. It's how I've come to recognize and acknowledge my shortcomings. It's how I've sorted out many a challenge. Lastly, writing is often my way of meditating on God's love. I live in the sunshine of his grace and know he understands, he cares, and leads me to an ever-brightening day.

My husband John recently suggested I put my writing "successes" together in a single volume. Compiling this book of personal-experience devotions, newspaper articles, essays, short stories of fiction, and even one poem (more like a jingle) has brought me great joy. I hope my family, friends, and all who read this book will find their spirits uplifted by *A Walk in the Sunshine*.

Helene Clare Kuoni

The path of the righteous is like the first gleam of dawn, shining ever brighter till the full light of day. ~ Proverbs 4:18 (NIV)

Note: Photographs included in this book did not appear with the material when originally published. They were added to enhance reader enjoyment of this compilation.

Bible Abbreviations:

GW	GOD's WORD Translation
KJV	King James Version
NIV	New International Version
NLT	New Living Translation

Solid Ground of God's Word

A Walk in the Sunshine

2 Kings 5:1-8 (NIV)

Now Naaman was commander of the army of the king of Aram. He was a great man in the sight of his master and highly regarded, because through him the LORD had given victory to Aram. He was a valiant soldier, but he had leprosy.

Now bands from Aram had gone out and had taken captive a young girl from Israel, and she served Naaman's wife. She said to her mistress, "If only my master would see the prophet who is in Samaria! He would cure him of his leprosy."

Naaman went to his master and told him what the girl from Israel had said. "By all means, go," the king of Aram replied. "I will send a letter to the king of Israel." So Naaman left, taking with him ten talents of silver, six thousand shekels of gold and ten sets of clothing. The letter that he took to the king of Israel read: "With this letter I am sending my servant Naaman to you so that you may cure him of his leprosy."

As soon as the king of Israel read the letter, he tore his robes and said, "Am I God? Can I kill and bring back to life? Why does this fellow send someone to me to be cured of his leprosy? See how he is trying to pick a quarrel with me!"

When Elisha the man of God heard that the king of Israel had torn his robes, he sent him this message: "Why have you torn your robes? Have the man come to me and he will know that there is a prophet in Israel."

Forwarding Mail[i]

I have written you quite boldly on some points, as if to remind you of them again, because of the grace God gave me to be a minister of Christ Jesus to the Gentiles. ~ Romans 15:15-16a (NIV)

A friend in Ohio recently sent me a journal from a West Coast schoolgirl. The journal, part of the girl's sixth-grade social studies project, is on a "journey" across the nation. The journal has already traveled to Oregon, Arizona, and Ohio. Each person who receives it is asked to write about the history and geography of his or her state. Unfortunately, my friend misplaced the journal, delaying its journey for more than two months. After I wrote a few pages, I gave it to my sister in New York, who plans to forward it to a friend in Minnesota. I hope that everyone will participate and speed it on its way!

In today's reading, a letter was sent to the king of Israel requesting that he heal Naaman, a leper. "Am I God?" the king rants upon reading the note. "Can I kill and bring back to life?" Then the king becomes suspicious, thinking the note was sent to begin a quarrel, as a precursor to an enemy invasion. Fortunately, the prophet Elisha learns about the letter and straightens everything out, and Naaman is healed. The letter's message reached the correct party.

The Bible is also like a letter – a message from God to us. It's not sent by mistake. God expects us to read it and learn from it. We should do so – and be quick to pass the message on to others!

Prayer: Heavenly Father, thank you for sending your Bible message to us and for entrusting us to pass it along. Keep us faithful in reading, applying, and sharing the Good News of salvation; in Christ. Amen

Genesis 7:1-3 (GW)

The LORD said to Noah, "Go into the ship with your whole family because I have seen that you alone are righteous among the people of today. Take with you seven pairs of every kind of clean animal (a male and a female of each) and one pair of every kind of unclean animal (a male and a female). Also, take seven pairs of every kind of bird (a male and a female of each) to preserve animal life all over the earth after the flood.

Touchdown![ii]

This is how you are to build it: The ark is to be 450 feet long, 75 feet wide and 45 feet high. ~ Genesis 6:15 (NIV)

My husband and I watched the football playoffs this weekend. Actually, John stared at the television screen, completely engrossed, but I didn't pay much attention. I was trying to read the book of Genesis. (I know this is not the best way to meditate on Scripture, but I wanted "togetherness time" with John, and I wanted to keep my New Year's resolution to read the Bible every day.)

Suddenly the crowd roaring in the stadium interrupted my reading. The quarterback caught the ball, tucked it neatly under his arm, and ran the whole length of the field.

"Do you realize," my husband asked, "how phenomenal that play was? He just ran from one end of the field to the other! He got through all the opponents' attempts to block!"

"How long is the field?" I asked.

"Three hundred feet."

"Interesting," I said. "Noah's ark was 450 feet long – the length of one and a half football fields!"

"No kidding?" John said. "That's huge!"

And that's how we both learned something new that afternoon.

I know, I shouldn't compromise my time with the Lord by reading Scripture in front of the TV. I'll try to do better in the future, but isn't it marvelous how the Lord's words can score a touchdown in spite of all the obstacles to block it?

Prayer: Thank you, Lord, for the relevance of your Word. Please bless even my most feeble attempts to draw closer to you; in Jesus' name. Amen

Psalm 1 (KJV)

Blessed *is* the man that walketh not in the counsel of the ungodly, nor standeth in the way of sinners, nor sitteth in the seat of the scornful.

But his delight *is* in the law of the LORD; and in his law doth he meditate day and night.

And he shall be like a tree planted by the rivers of water, that bringeth forth his fruit in his season; his leaf also shall not wither; and whatsoever he doeth shall prosper.

The ungodly *are* not so: but *are* like the chaff which the wind driveth away.

Therefore the ungodly shall not stand in the judgment, nor sinners in the congregation of the righteous.

For the LORD knoweth the way of the righteous: but the way of the ungodly shall perish.

Whose Leaf Does Not Wither[iii]

"If you obey my commands, you will remain in my love, just as I have obeyed my Father's commands and remain in his love." ~ John 15:10 (NIV)

We gave my aunt a 90th birthday party and the next day my sister took her on a week's vacation, stopping at my house for lunch the first day.

Aunt Lilly wore her corsage from the day before and carried a basket of flowers and a bouquet she'd received as gifts. We put the bouquet in water, but after lunch she wrapped up the flowers and took everything to my sister's home for overnight. The next day she carried all the flowers on the long drive to the mountains.

When they returned a week later and stopped by for lunch again, I was surprised to see that Aunt Lilly still wore her corsage, still carried all the flowers. The corsage was beautiful and the floral basket hearty. The bouquet was shedding, but nonetheless, we put it in water to keep for the journey's final lap.

How my aunt delighted in those flowers! In Psalm 1 the Lord promises to bless us if we delight in his law. If we remain in his love, he will keep us vibrant – vibrant as a fruit-bearing tree planted by streams of water. Vibrant as my aunt's flowers. Vibrant as Aunt Lilly at 90!

Prayer: Lord God, wondrous maker of heaven and earth, may we delight in your law, as my aunt delighted in the flowers you created. Help us to appreciate always all you have given us. Keep us vibrant as we study and meditate on your word; in Jesus' name. Amen

Genesis 3:1-4 (NIV)

Now the serpent was more crafty than any of the wild animals the LORD God had made. He said to the woman, "Did God really say, 'You must not eat from any tree in the garden'?"

The woman said to the serpent, "We may eat fruit from the trees in the garden, but God did say, 'You must not eat fruit from the tree that is in the middle of the garden, and you must not touch it, or you will die.'"

"You will not surely die," the serpent said to the woman.

Eve Misquoted

How can you say, "We are wise, for we have the law of the LORD," when actually the lying pen of the scribes has handled it falsely? ~ Jeremiah 8:8 (NIV)

A friend shared a book with me that he'd bought at the airport in Tel Aviv. It concerned Israel's postage stamps, specifically those based on Bible stories.

One stamp depicted the serpent tempting Eve in the Garden of Eden and the commentary given intrigued me. Though I was well familiar with the story, I'd never heard this particular interpretation.

It suggested that Eve gave the serpent the opportunity he was looking for when she misquoted God's instruction not to eat the fruit of a certain tree (the tree of the knowledge of good and evil). Because she said "…and you must not touch it…," the crafty serpent could prove those added words untrue and thereby gain her confidence. (Genesis 2:16-17)

Misquoting the Word of God can have terrible consequences. Yet, so many popular expressions are incorrectly ascribed to the Bible: "God helps those who help themselves," "Money is the root of all evil," "What goes around, comes around." I believe the Lord expects us to check the source frequently and guard against misquoting his Word. I believe Eve would agree.

Prayer: Lord, we may have been careless quoting Scripture in the past. Help us to do better, so that we accurately present – and represent – you, our God.

Read Your Bible
(A 50-word or less devotion on a question Jesus asked)

Question: *Jesus answered them, "Haven't you read what David did...?"*
~ Luke 6:3 (GW)

Devotion: Jesus is the living Word. And Scripture, the written Word. One message but two ways to know and experience the same love of God. Certainly, we would take both opportunities to draw close to such love! How awful it would be to hear Jesus' rebuke: "Don't you read the Scriptures?"

***

First Class Mail[iv]

All Scripture is God-breathed and is useful for teaching, rebuking, correcting and training in righteousness, so that the man of God may be thoroughly equipped for every good work. ~ 2 Timothy 3:16-17 (NIV)

Read Slowly. There is no rule that says you must get through the entire Bible in a year's time. Read every day, but read slowly, not only with your mind, but also with your heart. Remember: Read every word; God doesn't send junk mail.

Fair Days of Fellowship and Church

Psalm 84:1-4 (NIV)

How lovely is your dwelling place,
   O LORD Almighty!
My soul yearns, even faints,
   for the courts of the LORD;
my heart and my flesh cry out
   for the living God.
Even the sparrow has found a home,
   and the swallow a nest for herself,
   where she may have her young –
a place near your altar,
   O LORD Almighty, my King and my God.
Blessed are those who dwell in your house;
   they are ever praising you.

Hebrews 10:24-25 (NIV)

And let us consider how we may spur one another on toward love and good deeds. Let us not give up meeting together, as some are in the habit of doing, but let us encourage one another – and all the more as you see the Day approaching.

What's Really Broken?[v]

Ponder the path of thy feet, and let all thy ways be established.
~ Proverbs 4:26 (KJV)

I once fell on some ice and broke my elbow and wrist. In a bulky cast, I was unable to wear my winter coat for six weeks and became virtually homebound. Church friends came to visit or sent e-mail, keeping me informed of committee activities. I felt "connected" although I did not go to Sunday worship. After the cast was removed, I spent three weeks in a removable splint but continued to stay at home.

One day a box of flowers was delivered – a gift from a gal who had been homebound with a bad back. She'd returned to church the previous Sunday and heard someone request prayer for me as I was recovering from surgery on both feet! I don't know how that rumor started, but I knew it was time for me to return to church. Not only had I been unaware of the needs of someone with an injured back, but the congregation was praying for the wrong part of my anatomy!

It seems God was telling me to get up from the sofa and let my healthy feet carry me back into the fellowship of believers.

Prayer: Gracious Lord and Savior, help me not take lightly opportunities to worship you in the company of fellow believers. Thanks for those who "share with God's people who are in need" (Romans 12:13, NIV); in Jesus' name. Amen

2 Kings 2:11-13 (NIV)

As they were walking along and talking together, suddenly a chariot of fire and horses of fire appeared and separated the two of them, and Elijah went up to heaven in a whirlwind.

Elisha saw this and cried out, "My father! My father! The chariots and horsemen of Israel!" And Elisha saw him no more. Then he took hold of his own clothes and tore them apart.

He picked up the cloak that had fallen from Elijah and went back and stood on the bank of the Jordan.

The Mantle Passed

Remember the day you stood before the LORD your God at Horeb, when he said to me, "Assemble the people before me to hear my words so that they may learn to revere me as long as they live in the land and may teach them to their children." ~ Deuteronomy 4:10 (NIV)

I hurried through the old cemetery. The pathway zigzagged through the weatherworn gravestones and suddenly I heard faint singing. I quickened my pace. The music intensified. Finally, breathless, I arrived. I found my church already full that Sunday morning, the worship well under way.

Though the "shortcut" took longer than I'd expected, my route through the church cemetery provided a new perspective. Here "resting in peace" were the founding members of my congregation, those to whom I owed a debt of thanks. Many had lived over 200 years before and had been faithful. Today the sound of the bells in the steeple waft over their graves, and our congregation sings and rejoices in accord with their vision. Two centuries later God's people still gather in this place to praise the Lord.

Prayer: God of our fathers, thank you for the faithfulness of all who lived before us, who kept the faith and passed the message of your love down from generation to generation; in Jesus' name. Amen

1 John 4:1-6 (NIV)

Dear friends, do not believe every spirit, but test the spirits to see whether they are from God, because many false prophets have gone out into the world. This is how you can recognize the Spirit of God: Every spirit that acknowledges that Jesus Christ has come in the flesh is from God, but every spirit that does not acknowledge Jesus is not from God. This is the spirit of the antichrist, which you have heard is coming and even now is already in the world.

You, dear children, are from God and have overcome them, because the one who is in you is greater than the one who is in the world. They are from the world and therefore speak from the viewpoint of the world, and the world listens to them. We are from God, and whoever knows God listens to us; but whoever is not from God does not listen to us. This is how we recognize the Spirit of truth and the spirit of falsehood.

Condemned

My husband and I pass a beautiful church on our drive home from our summer vacations. We admire the magnificent architecture of the 150-year old building. But it is in terrible disrepair and abandoned. An official town sign hangs across the front door: "CONDEMNED!"

It breaks our hearts every time we go by. Though the exterior looks so majestic and inviting, the city building inspector has determined that it is unsafe to enter. Danger lurks behind the enticing façade.

To determine the condition of a building, code enforcement officers check the structure against a long list of conditions. By contrast, Christians have but a short list against which to test institutions for *spiritual integrity*.

We live in a world of many false prophets, but the Bible tells us how to test the spirits to see whether they are from God. *"Every spirit that acknowledges that Jesus Christ has come in the flesh is from God, but every spirit that does not acknowledge Jesus is not from God."* (1 John 4:2-3, NIV). All we have to do is ask that question whenever a new religious philosophy is presented to us.

Our heavenly Father cares for his children and warns us to be careful. Otherwise we might trust an institution that does not have Christ as its foundation, where danger is lurking, and where the "building" eventually will crumble and be condemned.

Prayer: Heavenly Father, you have given us a simple test and if we use it, we will stand on the firm footing of your love and teaching. Thank you, Lord Jesus. Amen

Amos 5:21-24 (NIV)

"I hate, I despise your religious feasts;
   I cannot stand your assemblies.
Even though you bring me burnt offerings and grain offerings,
   I will not accept them.
Though you bring choice fellowship offerings,
   I will have no regard for them.
Away with the noise of your songs!
   I will not listen to the music of your harps.
But let justice roll on like a river,
   righteousness like a never-failing stream!

Worship Styles[vi]

My husband and I drove home from church discussing the two worship styles we get to choose between each Sunday: contemporary and traditional. "Wish we could find a different name for the later service," John said. "Though 'contemporary' has a positive sound to it, the word 'traditional' connotes, to me, 'old-fashioned' or 'stuck-in-the-mud.'"

We considered several alternatives, then congratulated ourselves for coming up with a new label: "classical" worship. That word has a more positive ring. And, it describes the sophisticated language of the prayers, the rich poetry of the hymns, and the majesty of the anthems composed by the giants of classical music. Furthermore, folks who avoid "traditional" worship might actually be intrigued and challenged by "classical." Glad we solved that problem!

A few days later I came upon today's passage. What's this? God will not listen to our music no matter how lovely it is? I had to read further. The passage, I soon discovered, addresses our priorities, and once again I felt convicted!

I'm sure our little discussion about proper worship terminology was okay, but where was our discussion about establishing justice in the world and finding ways to do good? Doing good never goes out of style. It's traditional! It's contemporary! It's classic! It stands the test of time. The best worship is service; it's music to God's ears.

Prayer: Righteous God, you created the music of the spheres and put a love of music in our hearts. Make our desire for justice equally strong. Show us the many opportunities for doing good in the world, for this is the true worship you desire; in Jesus' name. Amen

Old-Fashioned Coffee Time
(Essay)

This morning I stood on the corner of Water and Pine, several coins sweating my palm. Only a few customers stood ahead of me and my turn came quickly.

The bagel vendor amazed me. Spending only seconds with each customer, he somehow gets acquainted. Yesterday he saw me later than usual. Today he asked, "Back on standard time?"

I smiled but simultaneously requested, "buttered cinnamon raisin." (Simultaneous talking is a survival technique in New York City. It is not rudeness as it would be deemed in other parts of the country. The folks queued up on street corners all over Manhattan appreciate this talent, because it doesn't delay the other folks on line who also have places to get to.)

I'm usually one of the fast-paced myself but this morning, having purchased my breakfast and having achieved my first supervisory duty of the day by arriving before the staff, I sat alone in my office, uncapped the Styrofoam cup of steaming coffee, and paused to reflect.

When I was a little girl, every so often on a Sunday afternoon my mother's mother came to visit for "coffee." She always dressed beautifully in a silk dress, usually black with splashes of floral print. She wore gloves, carried the black purse she'd crocheted herself, and topped off her outfit with a stylish hat fastened to her wispy hair with hatpins. In cool weather, she adorned her shoulders with a fur shawl. A fox fur full-body pelt, the tail at one end was gripped in the fox's teeth at the other. How soft it was to the touch.

Today I sat in my Manhattan office and sipped coffee as I pondered those long-ago Sunday visits. I remember waiting by our local library for Nana to arrive by public bus and when she did, I took her hand and escorted her home where Mom had the dining room ready. The table was covered with a lace cloth, the good china and silver. Flowers graced the center and cloth napkins were folded neatly by each plate.

Mom served the coffee and started the cake plates around the table. Everyone was so well-mannered and relaxed. There seemed time enough for style! My sisters and I drank our milk and I thought how I too would someday raise my pinky in the air and stir a sugar cube in a fine bone-china cup.

How lovely it was, but how different things are from what I'd dreamed. Today, elegance has come to mean a Styrofoam cup that does not leak. Style is being able to reach the phone without knocking over a Starbucks, drenching reports and computer runs.

I've become a working woman of the 20th century, but today I took five minutes to ponder that long-forgotten graciousness. I sense it's been lost forever in the name of speed and efficiency.

The Belfry[vii]

So Jacob set up a memorial, a stone marker, to mark the place where God had spoken with him. He poured a wine offering and olive oil on it.
~ Genesis 35:14 (GW)

A few years ago I visited Pittsburgh, PA. Strolling about the city, I came upon a curious tower – a tall grey-stone belfry on the corner of Fifth and Bellefield Avenues. It occurred to me, this might once have been the corner piece of a beautiful old church now gone. How sad, I thought, that only this remained.

As I considered the sleek office building now standing on the property, I thought: Great numbers of businesspeople walk past this belfry every day. Perhaps the tower stands as a reminder of those who once worshipped here.

Things change and people move on. Just as Jacob erected a pillar as a reminder to those who would come after him, the folks who had worshipped on this city corner also left a monument. It silently testifies to the fact that it was here God's people met with God, here that he spoke with them. The original building is gone, but the witness lives on.

Prayer: God of our fathers, thank you for the faithful witness of those who've gone before, who have strengthened the faith of many through the "reminders" they've left behind; in Jesus' name. Amen

[Note: Only the 1889 bell tower remains from the former Bellefield Presbyterian Church; is located in front of the University of Pittsburgh's Bellefield Towers Building.]

Remember Me

I visited a local historical museum to see an exhibit of samplers stitched by American schoolgirls in the late eighteenth century. During these years, life expectancy was short. The museum notes posted on the wall next to each example of needlework revealed that the 8- or 10-year old girl who worked the sampler, often did not live many years beyond its completion.

I felt stunned and deeply moved when I came upon a piece dated January 7, 1792. It simply asks: "When this you see, remember me. Chloe Jackson."

Two hundred years after the tiny fingers of an early American schoolgirl pushed a needle through this piece of linen, I stood in a museum, examined her fine work, and pondered the life of Chloe Jackson. I don't know how long she lived or what else she may have accomplished. Most probably, her life was quite ordinary at the time she stitched those words. The sampler could very well be the only evidence of her existence. Yet, I know one thing, she wanted to be remembered.

It was important to her. It is important to me. It's important to all who share the human experience. We want our lives to count. The desire to make a difference and to be remembered seems to have been woven at Creation into the very fabric of our being.

Jesus Christ, Savior of the World, redeemed mankind and changed the course of history. He rescued us from condemnation and promised us eternal life in Heaven. Yet, with great simplicity, he broke bread and asked us to "do this in remembrance of me." Contrary to our desire for fame, Christ's intentions were not vain-glorious. His request was for *our* benefit, for when we remember Jesus the gain is ours.

We have no idea why we should remember an obscure little Chloe Jackson, yet we've put her sampler in a museum for all to ponder. But to know and remember Jesus Christ brings life and brings it in abundance, now and forever. We must never put Jesus in a museum. We must "take and eat." (Matthew 26:26-30)

Dorothy's All-Time Favorite Carol[viii]
(Essay)

Let the heavens be glad, and the earth rejoice! Tell all the nations, "The LORD reigns!" ~ 1 Chronicles 16:31 (NLT)

"It's December 1," 12-year old Dorothy announced. "It's time to play Christmas music."

My older sister loved sitting at the sturdy upright, playing and singing her way through a frayed book of carols. I, three years younger, would hear her strike the first notes, rush to the sunporch, and join her on the piano bench. Sitting beside her and singing along, I'd plink the one-note melody line an octave higher. My part, though elementary, made me feel accomplished, and she seemed to enjoy the duet as much as I.

Our little fingers hammered out *O Come All Ye Faithful* and when we finished, she'd say, "That's my favorite." Then we would play *Hark, the Herald Angels Sing* and she'd declare, "That's my favorite." *I Heard the Bells on Christmas Day* elicited the same response, as did *The First Nowell*. It seemed every page of that tattered book of carols contained the one she liked best.

"But, Dorothy," I asked, "how can they all be your favorite?" She shrugged her shoulders and said, "Well, they just are." I, still a bit puzzled, shrugged my shoulders in reply and thought, *Okay.*

Dorothy never tried to be logical when it came to music. She just let it envelop her heart and imagination. She felt it. Enjoyed it. Reveled in it. Regardless of style – rhapsody, ragtime or hymn – she hit those ivories with a flourish.

Never mechanical, Dorothy played from the deepest reservoirs of her spirit. Yes, she read the notes, but she never bothered to count. That drove our piano teacher nuts. "Count. Ple-eeeze count!" Miss Lungen admonished, blood rushing to her head. But Dorothy would ask, "Would you please play it for me; how it should sound?" Miss Lungen always complied and demonstrated the proper rhythm right to the end of the music. When Dorothy tried again, Miss Lungen beamed. She felt triumphant, thinking my sister finally "got it." But clever Dorothy had simply mimicked what she'd heard Miss Lungen perform and she mimicked every detail perfectly.

No internal recitation of numbers cluttered Dorothy's brain. No! She kept her brain available to her imagination and what scenes and stories the tunes might conjure up. For instance, *Take Me Out to the Ballgame* transported Dorothy to Yankee Stadium where vendors, so impressed with her musicality, tossed everyone free hotdogs. And Dottie couldn't play *Anchors Aweigh* without blushing; a fleet of the Navy's most handsome sailors marched past the open sunporch windows and winked at her as they went by.

I, the logical one, never played music without a steady internal recitation: *1-2-3, 1-2-3...* And, as it turned out, it was a good thing for Dorothy that I did. When she was older and began to play church organ, she came to me to learn how to count. She now had a need to know, and I, though I didn't play as well as she, taught her the fine points of time notation found in a musical score.

Dorothy became an accomplished church musician. By nature quite shy, she found her voice at the three-manual console, her deft fingers commanding each keyboard, her leather-bottomed shoes confidently dancing across the pedals. Her love of the hymns – the melody and message of each – wafted out to the congregation as if on wings.

The Christmas Eve "service of lessons and carols" suited Dorothy particularly well. Since childhood, she had immersed herself in the repertoire of this season. Her passion for Christmas infused her playing with spirit. The tranquil sanctuary, window ledges bedecked with greenery, and a myriad of candles glowing, her soft prelude enhanced a mood of reverence and silent reflection. Then a designated reader opened the Bible to the familiar words of Luke chapter 2 and read, the congregation responding in song to each event of the narrative:

> *"... Augustus decreed that a census should be taken... All returned to their own ancestral towns to register... Because Joseph was a descendant of King David, he had to go to Bethlehem in Judea,... (Luke 2:1, 3-4, NLT)*

The reader paused; Dorothy played, and the congregation sang: *O Little Town of Bethlehem.*

The reader then returned to the lectern and continued the story:

> *"He traveled there from the village of Nazareth... He took with him Mary,... She gave birth to her first child, a son... and laid him in a manger... (Luke 2:4b, 5, 7, NLT)*

The reader returned to his seat as Dorothy played *Away in a Manger* and everyone sang.

So it continued, reader and organist alternating throughout the story. Dorothy led the singing from the organ bench, playing at the appropriate times: *It Came Upon the Midnight Clear* and *Angels, from the Realms of Glory.*

Finally, the readings concluded with:

> *"... All who heard... were astonished, but Mary kept all these things in her heart and thought about them often." (Luke 2:17-19, NLT)*

Dorothy played *What Child is This?*

Then, to conclude the worship, everyone sang the final carol, *Silent Night*. Ushers walked from pew to pew, lighting candles, and the flame was passed quickly among the congregation until the darkened sanctuary glowed. The pastor pronounced a benediction. Hushed and still, a sacredness permeated hearts throughout the assembly. But this "visit" to the manger, was not simply a holy respite from worldly matters. Worship had to resolve into joyous celebration. For God, creator of the universe, came in human form to save us from our sins. For this moment of triumph and hope, Dorothy used all the trumpet sounds available and introduced *Joy to the World*. With great abandon she let those organ pipes shake the rafters with a powerful rush of praise to the newborn king.

Dottie was 43 when illness kept her from her organ-playing responsibilities. She couldn't get to church, but "church" came to her when a hospital chaplain paid her a bedside visit. Learning of her music avocation, he asked, "How 'bout playing the mid-week Lenten service in the hospital chapel?" My sister's heart skipped.

A few days later, just twenty-four hours after undergoing major surgery, she helped the chaplain lead worship for other hospital patients. He wore his ministerial garb. She wore the new brushed velour bathrobe that my other sisters and I bought her for the occasion.

I thank Dorothy that my Christmas and Easter memories are so powerfully linked to her music. And it is impossible for me to sing the old Yuletide carols without shedding a tear in her memory.

Scripture says the events of earth are linked to events in heaven. Didn't the choir of angels flank the starry skies and herald Christ's birth on earth? Isn't there *"... joy in the presence of the angels of God over one sinner that repenteth"!* (Luke 15:10, KJV) The two realms are inexplicably intertwined.

For certain, Dorothy and I can no longer sit as children, side-by-side on the old piano bench. Nor can we fling wide the sunporch windows to entertain real or imagined passersby. But on Christmas Eve, when I'm part of the earthly chorus, I sense Dorothy is where the music lives in heaven. When creation is praising God around the globe this holy night, she and I sing carols together once again. Famous hymnist Isaac Watts understood and expressed it aptly when he penned: "And Heaven and nature sing" – lines from *Joy to the World*, Dorothy's favorite.

Sunrise of New Beginnings

Psalm 32:1-5 (GW)

Blessed is the person whose disobedience is forgiven
    and whose sin is pardoned.
Blessed is the person whom the LORD no longer accuses of sin
    and who has no deceitful thoughts.
When I kept silent about my sins,
    my bones began to weaken because of my groaning all day long.
Day and night your hand laid heavily on me.
My strength shriveled in the summer heat.
I made my sins known to you, and I did not cover up my guilt.
I decided to confess them to you, O LORD.
    Then you forgave all my sins.

Out of Kilter[ix]

People who conceal their sins will not prosper, but if they confess and turn from them, they will receive mercy. ~ Proverbs 28:13 (NLT)

We hired an electrician to install a pair of sconces on our dining room wall, one on either side of the china closet. After he'd worked awhile, I checked on his progress and immediately saw that the two lights were uneven.

"The left is higher than the right," I pointed out.

He put down his tools and came over to where I stood. Pondering his work from my perspective, he said, "Yeah, but no one will ever notice."

"No one will notice?" I responded, "I just did!"

Fortunately, he agreed to fix the problem.

How human it is to deny our wrongdoings, to cover up our faults! Are we like the electrician who needed to be confronted before correcting his error? Do we need to sense God's wrath before we confess our sins? I must admit I certainly did the very first time I acknowledged my shortcomings. Since then, however, I have learned that confession needs to be a part of our daily prayer. I work quickly to clear away all that hinders close fellowship with God, so that I can experience full joy in the Lord's presence, unhindered by unconfessed sin.

Prayer: Lord, along with King David in Psalm 32, I confess my transgressions to you, knowing that you forgive the guilt of my sin. Thank you in Jesus' name. Amen

Isaiah 55:6-9 (GW)

Seek the LORD while he may be found. Call on him while he is near.

Let wicked people abandon their ways. Let evil people abandon their thoughts. Let them return to the LORD, and he will show compassion to them. Let them return to our God, because he will freely forgive them.

"My thoughts are not your thoughts, and my ways are not your ways," declares the LORD.

"Just as the heavens are higher than the earth, so my ways are higher than your ways, and my thoughts are higher than your thoughts."

Loss and Gain[x]

"Those who want to save their lives will lose them. But those who lose their lives for me will save them." ~ Luke 9:24 (GW)

I was easily offended when I was a child. I took everything personally and often felt hurt when no offense was intended. A classmate often infuriated me; every time I objected to something she said, she'd retort, "Oh, Helene, you're too sensitive." Flailing that phrase at me was tantamount to waving a red flag in front of a bull. It really caused me to charge.

One day in prayer, I faced the truth of my self-centered nature and confessed my "touchiness" to God. I repented of my "thin skin" and asked the Lord to change my nature. I earnestly desired to bury that part of my personality. God answered my prayer almost overnight and I no longer was quick to take offense. But the change he wrought surprised me. My sensitive nature didn't go away. It simply "died to self" and was reborn in increased sensitivity and empathy to other people and their feelings.

Prayer: Lord, help me to surrender those parts of my life that stand in the way of my service to you, and convert them for your glory; in Jesus' name. Amen

Green, but Not Growing

You know my folly, O God; my guilt is not hidden from you.
~ Psalm 69:5 (NIV)

After no rain for months, the radio station's meteorologist announced: "This is the worst drought in 30 years. Every lawn has turned yellow, every well has dried up, and the heat and humidity are responsible for several deaths."

I listened carefully, hoping the weather forecaster would predict rain. Instead he reported that Highway Department crews, with buckets and brushes in hand, were busy on the major roadways. Out on the median dividers, they were painting the brown grass green.

I saw it later when I was driving and must admit the green paint job made things look better – but it didn't solve the underlying problem. Furthermore, I don't believe many people were fooled.

God is not fooled either, when we try to make ourselves look good, when we gloss over our real nature. God knows the truth, and when we admit our real condition, he will give us a fresh start. How foolish it is to try to camouflage our spiritual drought, when God is ready to shower us with blessings.

Prayer: Thank you God, for inviting us to the fountain of salvation. You alone can revive and refresh us with the living water that is Jesus Christ; in his name we pray. Amen

The Key to Undoing[xi]

If we claim to be without sin, we deceive ourselves and the truth is not in us. If we confess our sins, he is faithful and just and will forgive us our sins and purify us from all unrighteousness. ~ 1 John 1:8-9 (NIV)

Isn't the "undo" key on the computer a wonderful feature? With a click of the mouse, I can make my latest mistake disappear as if it had never happened, that is, if I press "undo" immediately. If I'm slow in discovering my error and make intervening keystrokes before I hit the "undo," well, that's just too bad. Correcting the mistake will take a lot more time and effort. It's as if a flippant computer callously said, "Too late! That's life!"

Come to think of it, that is life. That's exactly how it works. If we catch our errors right away, it's so much simpler to make amends and go forward. But what a job getting back on track if the error goes undetected or worse yet, compounds.

What a loving God we have who established the Law and makes it known to us, for his law is our early detection system. But he didn't just give us the law to catch us at every mistake. God is merciful and also gives us the key to recovery, the key Jesus preached known as "repentance," the "undo" key of life.

Best of all, God is not unfeeling like the cold nuts and bolts of my computer. He'll never say, "Too bad! Too late!" Though he desires we come early and escape the escalation of our errors and the time spent in recovery, it's never too late to know his forgiveness and the life he bestows in abundance. Yes, with the Lord's "undo," we'll produce a new manuscript – a new life, full of God's richest blessings.

Sun, Moon, and Stars – God's Faithfulness in Nature

Remain True
(A 50-word or less devotion on a question Jesus asked)

Question: *Jesus' speech made many of his disciples go back to the lives they had led before they followed Jesus. So Jesus asked the twelve apostles, "Do you want to leave me too?"* ~ John 6:66-67 (GW)

Devotion: How powerful the pull of the crowd! From birth, we imitate those around us – to learn, to grow. It's powerful behavior and works to our benefit. But when we're no longer children, we must choose for ourselves whom to follow. Imitating Jesus will lead us to everlasting joy.

***

Trustworthy Timbers[xii]

The lamp of the LORD searches the spirit of a man; it searches out his inmost being. ~ Proverbs 20:27 (NIV)

When my husband John went to the attic to lay some flooring, I brought him a lamp so he wouldn't have to work in the dark.

We turned on the light and discovered the manufacturer's trademark on the roof planks. To our surprise and delight, the wood used to build our New Jersey house had come from John's home state of Oregon, and from a lumber mill he knew well.

When the Lord turns on his lamp to search my spirit, to see the timbers with which I'm built, I pray he finds the manufacturer's mark clearly visible, and the imprint is his own.

Beauty Secrets[xiii]

My friend's little boy sat with his family and watched the Miss America contest on TV. Snuggled up on the couch with his grandmother, he stared with fascination as each finalist walked down the runway, competing for the title and crown.

His mom, his dad, and his older sister each named the contestant they admired most. Not to be outdone, Mikey said he had a favorite too. With twinkling eyes he shot an admiring glance to his closest companion. "It's Grandma," he said. "She's the most beautiful!"

The family chuckled, but his dad agreed. "Mikey's right," he said. "People need to age a bit to become beautiful."

The pageant contestants were all pretty, and all attired in the finest clothes. Each had invested significant time and money preparing for the day. They were stunning for sure, but they were just too young to be called "beautiful."

Grandma's beauty is by far superior, the kind that cannot be acquired, or applied from the outside. It comes gradually, over a lifetime. It comes from within, the by-product of trusting and living in a close relationship with the Lord.

The Bible tells us that King Solomon possessed the best of everything, yet even with his crown and regal attire he did not have the beauty of a lily in the field – a lily whose beauty secret, and Grandma's, is simply to live and to grow according to the purpose intended for it by God.

Hold Fast to Your Faith[xiv]

If a prophet… announces to you a miraculous sign or wonder, and if the sign or wonder of which he has spoken takes place, and he says, "Let us follow other gods" (gods you have not known) "and let us worship them," you must not listen… The LORD your God is testing you to find out whether you love him with all your heart and with all your soul. It is the LORD your God you must follow, and him you must revere. Keep his commands and obey him; serve him and hold fast to him.
~ Deuteronomy 13:1-4 (NIV)

I went to my violin lesson feeling fully prepared, but it seemed my teacher expected better. She wasn't impressed that I played all the right notes or sustained each for the time count indicated in the score. She wanted to see proper bowing, confident fingering, and, worst of all, she wanted to hear expression. Then to challenge me further, she played her violin at the same time – but not in unison. She played a discordant harmony, making it even more difficult for me to hear and keep true to the proper pitch.

"I sounded much better before I came to class," I finally said, exasperated.

"No," she replied, "don't say that! It does you no good to say you played it better before coming." Seeing she had my attention, she added this punch line: "You play the music only as well as you play it under pressure. You must not let me, or what I play, distract you."

On the walk home across campus, I considered her words. How true that is in our relationship with God as well. We can feel over-confident, or even smug about our faith in God as long as we're performing our daily routines; they are mechanical. The challenge comes when others try to introduce us to false teachings. When this happens, the steadfastness of our faith is tested. Will we remain true to Christ?

It's wise to remember this: faith is only as strong as it is under pressure.

Sun, Moon, and Stars – God's Faithfulness in Nature   41

When college, and life after college, introduces difficult "music," we want our faith to hold secure, grow strong, and produce a symphony of praise to his glory. Then we'll be able to say with joy: *"My feet have closely followed his steps; I have kept to his way without turning aside."* (Job 23:11, NIV)

Faithful in One Concern

I am saying this for your own good, not to restrict you, but that you may live in a right way in undivided devotion to the Lord. ~ 1 Corinthians 7:35 (NIV)

My friend Janice takes her guitar to a senior care facility every Wednesday. She plays choruses, shares a devotional message, and leads the residents in prayer. She promises to return in a week's time and suggests activities for everyone to do in the meantime. She lists Bible verses to memorize and requests prayer for various people with specific concerns.

"Pray for Mary," she'll say. "She's having trouble with her eyesight." And "Pray for Jake; his arthritis is bothering him." Down the list she goes, giving each name and specific need.

One day Janice gazed up from her list and saw a woman crying. "What's wrong?" she asked. "You give us so many people to pray for. And so many Bible verses to memorize. It's too much for me."

"Oh, you don't have to do everything," Janice replied. "Choose one verse or one person." The distressed resident relaxed, confident she could handle that.

The Lord made things simple for Adam and Eve in the Garden. He gave them just one command. Furthermore, it wasn't an assignment for them to accomplish; it was something they should avoid doing. How much easier could it have been? Even so, they disobeyed.

Sometimes, the Lord impresses upon us something we should get busy and do. We wake up in the morning, knowing there is one thing that's important to accomplish that day. Or perhaps there is something we must endeavor to avoid that day. I've discovered it's always best to start the day with prayer, asking the Lord to keep us faithful and obedient. We are human and know we can easily fail – even when there's only one concern.

Prayer: Lord, be near, help me focus on those activities you would have me do this day. Amen

Fickle? Me?

"... Your love is like the morning mist, like the early dew that disappears." ~ Hosea 6:4 (NIV)

My folks once visited a "long-lost" cousin who lived a distance away, meeting her and her family for the first time. They enjoyed a pleasant afternoon together, and as they were saying goodbye, my mom complimented the young mother on her three beautiful children. Then she turned to the youngest, about four years old, and said, "You're cute as a button! Would you like to come home with me?"

The boy turned and ran off to his bedroom and everyone chuckled. But a few minutes later he returned with his suitcase! We never did figure out if this was an early sign of an adventurous spirit, a budding sense of humor, or a fickle personality.

Fickle? That's an old-fashioned word we don't hear much anymore. Yet, it's a problem today, because this generation seems plagued with short attention spans, and short-lived allegiances. We flit from one thing to the next, seeking immediate gratification, but this is not the Lord's way. His promises run contrary to popular culture and he promises us a crown of life if we remain faithful until the end. (Revelation 2:10)

Prayer: Faithful Lord, I do not want to "pack my bags" and follow every new voice that comes along. I want to be faithful to your word and your leading; in Jesus' name. Amen

Daily Steps

In his heart a man plans his course, but the LORD determines his steps.
~ Proverbs 16:9 (NIV)

Life, at times, seems focused on meaningless routine. We want our lives to count for something noble, but each day seems taken up with waking, dressing, eating, trudging off for the morning commute, running errands on the way home. We handle the dreary details and hope God sees the larger picture, right?

That's what I always thought, but today's verse tells me otherwise. We can envision the dream, the goal, but God will determine the details of our course.

If life seems dreary, perhaps we do not hold a big enough dream in our hearts. The bigger the dream, the more exciting life becomes. Sometimes the steps God provides are not the ones we'd anticipate. Sometimes they are "course-corrections." Sometimes they prove time-consuming and tedious, and in our short-sighted view might even appear to be obstacles. When I remember that my steps are determined by God, they drive me on to the goal and even the steps that are routine take on a noble purpose.

Those who followed the Oregon Trail in the mid-1800s, literally walked across the country. They took one step at a time. They knew the goal and with the big dream in their hearts, they successfully reached their destination.

Prayer: Lord, be near me this day that even the common, routine steps I take are pleasing to you.

Wise Investments[xv]

"... You earn wages, only to put them in a purse with holes in it."
~ Haggai 1:6 (NIV)

My grandfather came from Europe in the early 1900s. At 14 years old he found employment washing dishes. He worked hard, put in long hours, and applied himself to learning how to make candy and ice cream. His efforts were blessed with success and soon he had a number of ice cream stores, an ice cream cone factory, and other small businesses.

He made money because he worked so hard. But when he had acquired a measure of wealth, friends and acquaintances began asking for loans. He was kind and generous and, as far as I know, he refused no one. But many of the "purses" he helped fill had holes in them and the money was not repaid.

I look around my house and see the many possessions I've acquired through the years. I've used and enjoyed many of them but some represent foolish purchases, have never been used and serve only to collect dust. I've worked hard but I must admit I've put some of my earnings into "purses" with holes.

As I think back over the challenges of my career, I recall the many times I went to God for his wisdom, his strength, his presence on-the-job. He was kind and generous in response to my requests for his help. I pray now that he help me to use well all that he has invested in me, that I do not prove to be a "purse" with holes.

Prayer: O Lord, you have given me assets, and blessed me with talents. But your greatest investment in me was when you died on the cross. Help me to honor your trust, to use all your blessings wisely, and to bear much fruit for your kingdom; in Jesus' name. Amen

Keeping the Faith

Sunday morning at the Bronx Veterans Administration Hospital is a quiet time. Friends, families, hospital workers and volunteers help patients out of bed or up from their chairs and accompany them down the corridor to the elevators. Several are pushed in wheelchairs. A few need another's arm for balance as they walk. Some shuffle on their own.

Oh so slowly they make their way down one corridor, then the next. It seems they will never make their destination on time. But each knows the routine and how long their individual trip takes. The pilgrimage is made by men and women of all races, all ages, all physical conditions, most in bathrobes and slippers, some in metal braces and head frames.

When they come through the chapel doors, they trade the low hospital ceilings and windowless corridor walls for a high vaulted roof and sunshine that streams long beams of light through stained glass. The center aisle, carpeted in red, is wide, and some worshipers simply park their vehicles right there. The bells and buzzers, the speaker system and the scratchy, squealy sounds of equipment on linoleum tile is forgotten. Entering worshipers are met by new sounds – the soft, soothing, healing tones of an organist's prelude. They have come to draw near to God.

The Protestant Chaplain, the Reverend William Gillies Kalaidjian, enters in his black academic robe, and the service begins with silent prayer. Each head that can, is bowed. All eyes are closed in silent meditation. Each person communes with his Maker in solitude, and no one knows all the thoughts that rise to heaven in that sacred moment. If any count blessings, there must be at least one prayer of gratitude for the chapel itself. The Lord spared the sanctuary from demolition; He enabled Chaplain Bill to champion that cause.

His congregants know the man well: his broad frame; his extra full face and square jawline; the wiry salt and pepper hair he parts slightly right of center. They know his eyes, which twinkle with impish charm when he shares a joke. Yet that royal blue can turn steel when injustice demands it.

He visits often. He prays at every bedside. He chats; he counsels, and he attacks doom and gloom in a head-on style all his own. He cuts through superfluous flab and gets to the heart as quickly as a flinty scalpel. His words are earnest. His barking tends to ingratiate, not offend, and even at times, to evoke laughter.

"What's that you've got there?" he might bellow, as he enters a patient's room. "The *Daily News*? You've read all the bad news. No wonder you're depressed. Here's a Bible, so you can read the Good News."

The paper falls from the knees and a spotted, palsied hand draws circles in the air, which translated mean, "Come sit a bit. You're welcome here." Together, they turn to the Psalms.

> *The LORD is my light and my salvation –*
> *Whom shall I fear?*
> *The LORD is the stronghold of my life –*
> *Of whom shall I be afraid?...*
> *Wait for the LORD, be strong and take heart*
> *and wait for the LORD.* ~ (Psalm 27:1, 14, NIV)

The chaplain's hands are large, and, at once, both soft and strong. It is as if two Yankee catcher's mitts are wrapped around the old man's hands, and they pray.

When patients are able, they get to services to hear this pastor preach, this man who was instrumental in saving their chapel a dozen years ago. In 1978 the Veterans Administration office in Washington announced plans to expand the Bronx facility. A new hospital was needed, and the improvements were welcomed, but one phase of the project was a "mixed bag." To create 20 additional parking spaces in the visitor's lot, the church was to be brought down.

That was more than Kalaidjian would tolerate. The VA chapel was not some small room with 9-foot ceiling, tucked away in an unused alcove. It was a magnificent old, red brick building with slate tiles on the roof and was large enough to seat 700. Its interior pillars formed stately arches that met the vaulted ceiling high above the nave. Stained glass adorned the front and side aisles and a rose window graced the choir loft in the rear.

The church stood on the site of George Washington's old Fort Number 6. It was the work of noted architect Stanford White, built in 1901 for the Roman Catholic Orphan Asylum that was there at the time. The first congregation of several hundred schoolboys was strikingly different from the one that gathers there now.

Today Protestants, Catholics and Jews feel equally comfortable because of a unique "three-faiths altar." With the press of a button, the platform turns, and within minutes the sanctuary is transformed for the traditions of whatever group is assembled. It was the gift of New York's *Journal American* in 1951, the newspaper's memorial to the four chaplains of different creeds who gave their life jackets to other men, joined hands, and went down with the sinking S.S. Dorchester, on February 3, 1944.

For Chaplain Bill, destroying a place so rich in history and beauty and so full of meaning to all who worshipped there was tantamount to sacrilege. Descended from the Armenian race, a people made strong by adversity and persecution, and coming from the hard-working stock of his own family line, Kalaidjian is no stranger to "blood, sweat and tears." Knowing something is wrong and wanting to make it right, he rolls up his sleeves and gets to work.

He had, over the years, headed other campaigns. As minister of Bedford Park Congregational Church (Bronx, NY), he once led a public outcry against vagrants and drunkards who lived on Mosholu Parkway's median divider. As the Senior Chaplain to the NYPD, he often went to bat for a cop. As president of the Bronx Society for the Prevention of Cruelty to Children, he testified on many occasions to save a child from abuse. As General Secretary for the Armenian National Sanitarium in Lebanon, he travelled to Beirut in '77, to deliver financial aid and was the target of a political kidnap attempt. Strong, determined, forceful? For sure, but the VA bureaucracy was fiercely unyielding.

He wrote, he called, he confronted. He put together a coalition of Catholic, Protestant, and Jewish religious leaders. He enlisted the support of the American Legion, the Catholic War Veterans, the Jewish War Veterans, and the Veterans of Foreign Wars.

He prayed morning and evening and kept his pen in motion. He wrote Councilwoman Aileen Ryan, Walter Hoving at the Metropolitan Museum of Art, and Jackie Onasis on Fifth Avenue. He wrote to the Bronx Historical Society, the Bronx Women's Club, the Federation of Women's Clubs of Greater New York, and the Kingsbridge Historical Society, urging supporters to sign petitions and to write to the VA in Washington and to U.S. Senators Moynihan and Javits.

He wrote to the National Conference of Christians and Jews:

> "In a day and age when materialism and greed and prejudice are still very evident, let us consider saving a symbol in our midst that preserves the past in all its beauty – a visible testimony to the sacred in life and the Source of all healing."

"This chapel is a symbol of unity under God," he told the *Daily News*. "It portrays a loving spirit."

In early 1978, Assemblyman George Friedman of the 83rd A.D. introduced a resolution in Albany that congress take steps to prevent the demolition. He said, "The chapel serves as a place for prayer, solace, and contemplation for all faiths." The New York State Assembly voted its approval unanimously.

Every time his efforts appeared to produce some good, it seemed Kalaidjian's path would cross that of his nemesis, one of his fellow chaplains, Rabbi Leeman.

Leeman would tell him he was fighting a losing battle or remind him he was getting too many people upset. One day he warned, "If you don't watch out, you'll lose your job."

The remark provoked Bill. "Compared to how I feel about that chapel," Kalaidjian, now devoid of patience, snapped back, "I don't give two hoots for this job. That's just how I feel."

Though he was feeling the strain, he kept writing, and his writing encouraged others to do the same. Veteran Seymour Alper wrote to the Editor of the *Riverdale Press*. His letter appeared on February 2, 1978:

> "... Why the Chapel? This building is where many a moment of truth was faced for so many veterans and their loved ones. No one goes to a hospital for a vacation. You either get well and recover or meet your Maker. Thus a chapel for those troubled with illness and old war wounds is meaningful... As one who prayed there I can feel that attachment one has for it. It is no ordinary building, nor an ordinary chapel. It cannot be replaced with a new one or a better one. It just cannot be replaced – it can only be destroyed... Perhaps a hospital is so concerned with saving lives, it has forgotten what it is saving lives for..."

Kalaidjian's campaign drew more support as word spread, but in spite of increased press coverage, the VA plans remained unchanged. Many questioned whether his prayers would be answered, but he persisted.

One day, Washington's Chief of Veterans Affairs was sent to tour the New York facilities and Reverend Bill hosted the outing. The day was strenuous and humbling, for the middle-aged chaplain was asked to lift Max Clelland from his wheelchair and hoist him up into the helicopter. Max was a heavy man, even without the three limbs he lost in Vietnam.

Sun, Moon, and Stars – God's Faithfulness in Nature   51

Together, they flew high above the Big Apple, down the East River to Brooklyn and Queens, then up the Hudson and over the George Washington Bridge. It had to be like this, this madcap excursion by air. It was the only way Max could see the locations on his agenda in the time allotted. They covered the five boroughs, took a quick hop over the Empire State Building, and finally touched down at the VA Hospital in the Bronx; both men were exhilarated but physically beat.

Bill sensed Clelland's awe as he wheeled him into the chapel but spent from months of fruitless struggle and the demands of the day, the chaplain had no fight left. He put it to Max simply: "Why must the Bronx be stripped of everything good?"

Clelland was silent for a moment as he took in the wide aisles, the stone pillars and the stained-glass windows. "They'll not touch THIS chapel!" he replied, and with such fervency that the chaplain knew he could count on it. It cost many hours of writing, telephoning, pleading, persuading, and prayer. The reward had arrived in this hour.

The chapel was renovated, and on Veterans Day, November 11, 1988, the Protestant, Catholic, and Jewish chaplains rededicated this unique house of worship. Ten years earlier, the chapel had been scheduled for demolition to accommodate 20 additional parking spaces, but clergy of all backgrounds, legislators, civic and veterans associations had banded together and fought to save the church. Now they were gathered together to rededicate the Lord's temple, "a house of prayer for all people."

The clergy sat together, among them Rabbi Leeman. Each participated in turn, as the service progressed through invocation, prayers, and the Psalm. Chaplains Dwyer, Krantz, and Friederich presented the Catholic, Jewish and Protestant altars, and Chaplain William Gillies Kalaidjian, who had given so much of himself to save a magnificent chapel for others, lead the prayer of dedication:

> "We now, the veteran community, its members and friends, mindful of the goodness of government and the greatness of the people of the United States, cherish the

inheritance of this chapel, all it has meant down through the years, all it means to us this day, and for all it will mean to future generations. We are part of the glorious company of the seen and unseen. We recognize how deeply we are bound to the Lord of life and to each other, and we covenant together in this act of rededication, offering ourselves anew to the worship and work of a God who knows who we are and what we need."

He looked up, over the heads of those facing him in the congregation and studied the circular window in the choir loft. It was a stained-glass work of art, and its focus was the Holy Spirit, represented as a dove. He thought of the devoted Sisters of Charity and the orphan boys, who, during the First World War, had thought they might lose their property to the war effort and had spent their summer evenings in prayer not to be torn away from their home and their chapel.

Then, in 1921, when the government bought the property for a new VA Hospital, the men and women of the Roman Catholic Orphan Asylum bid farewell to their church, praying that the Holy Spirit would always remain – to console, to forgive, to enlighten, to sanctify.

Reverend Bill's thoughts turned to his own strenuous efforts, which had seemed futile for so long, and to the madcap helicopter tour that had drained him and made further effort impossible. This was the day he rested from the struggle. This was the day his prayers were answered. This was the day the chapel was saved.

Wait for the LORD; be strong and take heart and wait for the LORD.
~ Psalm 27:14 (NIV)

Fog of Fear and Indecision

Me – At Age Three

Try as I might, I couldn't get it off my feet. I shuffled when I walked, scraped my soles on the pavement, jumped, kicked, twisted and turned, even squealed at it but nothing worked. Finally, my mommy crossed me over to the shady side of the street and it disappeared.

But my fears kept me out of the sunshine.

The Timeless Message of Love

But now, this is what the LORD says – he who created you, O Jacob, he who formed you, O Israel: "Fear not, for I have redeemed you; I have summoned you by name; you are mine." ~ Isaiah 43:1 (NIV)

Ken, a new Christian in our Bible study group, comes directly from his job and returns to his office immediately after we meet. His curious co-workers recently asked him what he is learning at our study.

He replied, "Bottom line – Jesus says, 'Don't be afraid.'"

Ken's been impressed with the number of times Jesus says these or similar words in the New Testament book of Mark. Ken hears the Lord speaking these words to him personally, to be confident of his salvation and to be assured of God's help when he struggles with life's challenges.

God's message "Fear not" appears throughout Scripture – throughout both the Old and New Testaments. God's love is so great that he paid the price of the cross to redeem us. Our salvation is sure. He is with us always. We need not, and must not, give in to fear.

Prayer: Lord, I will not fear with you beside me.

Courage in C Major
(Fiction Short Story)

The message read, "Call Dr. Stone." Still wearing my snow-covered boots, and tasting the lunch I'd swallowed whole, I collapsed into my desk chair. My co-worker Janet had delivered the note with such urgency, I knew she'd experienced Stone's wrath in my absence.

"Who," she asked, "is Dr. Stone? Or maybe I should say, who does he think he is?"

"My music professor," I answered.

"Oh, that's Dr. Stone." Her face brightened, now understanding all the frightening tales I'd told her.

"Shouldn't a music course be enjoyable?" She sat studying my face and I nodded.

When I'd enrolled, I believed music would provide a nice change from my 40-hour work week of computers, numbers, symbols and codes. I needed to relax. But with the bliss of an ignorant autumn leaf falling from bough to bonfire, I registered for this evening course with the "Terror of Union College."

I suppose I could have dropped out but the idea of quitting appalled me. I'm a compulsive problem solver and I find no peace in giving up, no matter how unpleasant the dilemma.

So last class I'd volunteered to pick up some music on my lunch hour, thinking that by doing the old bully this favor, I might establish a new rapport with him.

The snow fell and the wind gusted, as I boarded the Fifth Avenue bus that took me to Cooper Square and Carl Fischer Music Store. The bus inched its way downtown to avoid skidding and I, the sole passenger, stared over the driver's shoulder, mentally helping him see through the icy windshield.

I absently swallowed my sandwich, and though it took light-years, we made the trip safely.

I dashed into the store, grabbed the recital piece for Stone and met the same bus, now turned around for the trip uptown. The return trip was no less treacherous. But now I feared not only the slick roadway but Dr. Stone's short temper. Opening the package on my lap, I discovered I had bought the wrong arrangement. Too late to turn back. Not only had I gone past my lunch time, but the clerk at Carl Fischer's had locked its doors behind me, closing early because of the storm. The recital was that night and I had the wrong music. I just knew the professor would burst apart when he heard.

Now back in the office and holding the note my co-worker handed me, I reached for the phone but hesitated. As if she could sense my cowardice, Janet startled me. "Remember," she said, "if you learn to face the music, you may someday lead the band."

I grabbed the receiver, knowing my resolve would last only so long. Mrs. Smithers, Stone's chatty secretary answered on the first ring and my heart sank. I knew if she didn't let me speak with him soon, I'd lose my courage.

"You poor dear," she began. "You went out in this weather and all. Take vitamin C. My niece, the one in Michigan, caught pneumonia last year in the middle of the summer, would you believe? They have a place on the lake. Cost them a fortune. But it's none of my business how they throw their money away. And Ellie, that's my sister, she was against the marriage too."

"Mrs. Smithers, please," I interrupted.

Jolted back to the present moment, she continued. "My dear, oh yes, how can I tell you after all the trouble you've gone to? The recital has been cancelled. Dr. Stone called your office earlier but you were already on your lunch hour, tracking down the score in this terrible weather. He's been dreading your call. Made me promise I'd talk to you. He was afraid to tell you."

"He was afraid to tell me?" I was astounded.

"Yes," she said. "Between you and me, he's been a nervous wreck about it. You know, he'll never be appointed department chair as much as he craves the position. He just can't cope when things go wrong."

As I said goodbye, I sank back into my chair, totally mystified but thoroughly relieved. I even began to feel smug – that though one of us was a coward, it wasn't me.

Janet's face was a question mark. But we shared a good laugh when I said, "Would you believe it, the maestro has never learned to face the music!"

Refreshing Times of Friendship

2 Samuel 12:15-23 (NIV)

After Nathan had gone home, the LORD struck the child that Uriah's wife had borne to David, and he became ill. David pleaded with God for the child. He fasted and went into his house and spent the nights lying on the ground. The elders of his household stood beside him to get him up from the ground, but he refused, and he would not eat any food with them.

On the seventh day the child died. David's attendants were afraid to tell him that the child was dead, for they thought, "While the child was still living, we spoke to David but he would not listen to us. How can we tell him the child is dead? He may do something desperate."

David noticed that his attendants were whispering among themselves, and he realized the child was dead. "Is the child dead?" he asked.

"Yes," they replied, "he is dead."

Then David got up from the ground. After he had washed, put on lotions and changed his clothes, he went into the house of the LORD and worshiped. Then he went to his own house, and at his request they served him food, and he ate.

His servants asked him, "Why are you acting this way? While the child was alive, you fasted and wept, but now that the child is dead, you get up and eat!"

He answered, "While the child was still alive, I fasted and wept. I thought, 'Who knows? The LORD may be gracious to me and let the child live.' But now that he is dead, why should I fast? Can I bring him back again? I will go to him, but he will not return to me."

Friendship Helps[xvi]

The elders of his household stood beside him to get him up from the ground, but he refused... ~ 2 Samuel 12:17 (NIV)

Betty refused to be consoled when her mother died. She shed bitter tears every night for a year and a half, and even announced that she would weep daily for the rest of her life. We, her friends, tried to comfort her in every way we could, but she refused our help. We felt frustrated, and at times impatient, but we continued to pray for her. Finally, Betty began to focus on life again.

I am convinced more than ever that in disappointment, sickness, failure, or heartbreak, there's nothing like having others stand by us – especially those who share our faith in Christ. But friends can't do the job alone. It takes a conscious decision to accept their friendship, even though in the depths of despair the help offered always seems insufficient. When we accept the aid of friends, small and inadequate though it might be, the Lord begins his work of healing. And we know he will stand by us, for he is our very best friend.

Prayer: Lord, thank you for friends who remain faithful in times of need. Help me to see that their steadfastness is a gift from you; in Jesus' name. Amen

Jeremiah 9:23-24 (NLT)

This is what the LORD says: "Don't let the wise boast in their wisdom, or the powerful boast in their power, or the rich boast in their riches. But those who wish to boast should boast in this alone: that they truly know me and understand that I am the LORD who demonstrates unfailing love and who brings justice and righteousness to the earth, and that I delight in these things. I, the LORD, have spoken!"

Galatians 6:14 (NIV)

May I never boast except in the cross of our Lord Jesus Christ, through which the world has been crucified to me, and I to the world.

Bragging Rights[xvii]

...the tongue is a small part of the body, but it makes great boasts...
~ James 3:5 (NIV)

I enjoy saying that I was once on stage at Carnegie Hall, the place famous for great musicians. It's fun to see my friends' eyebrows raised in admiration and curiosity. Then I quickly explain that my high school held its graduation exercises there and that 669 of us seniors marched across the stage to receive our diplomas.

I also tell of being on stage with celebrated pianist Van Cliburn. That too gets a reaction. Truth was that the theater tickets had been oversubscribed, so chairs were placed on stage to accommodate the overflow audience.

How easy it is to brag a little (even though I always admit the complete story and get a laugh)! My little boasts put me temporarily in the company of great people. The apostle Paul felt no such need for greatness. He said, "May I never boast except in the cross of our Lord Jesus Christ" (Galatians 6:14, NIV). His "claim to fame," unlike mine, was neither silly nor temporary. Paul's boast was profound and had eternal consequence.

Prayer: Lord, help me to reorganize my priorities. My goal should not be to achieve human recognition but to bring you pleasure; in Jesus' name. Amen

True Friends

May the Lord be merciful to the family of Onesiphorus. He often took care of my needs and wasn't ashamed that I was a prisoner.
~ 2 Timothy 1:16 (GW)

A friend loves at all times... ~ Proverbs 17:17 (NIV)

After a weekend of painting and wallpapering, my husband and I still had not finished the job. Paint cans, drop cloths, and ladders cluttered the living and dining rooms, not to mention that the furniture was "camped out" in all the wrong places. But in spite of the sanding dust and overall mess, we decided to host our regular Bible study group.

Our friends arrived and shared in the excitement of the plans we had for our dream dining room. Then we prayed together and continued our study of Genesis. At the end of the evening, the gal who led us in the concluding prayer surprised me. She thanked the Lord for our hospitality – in our "beautiful home."

I thank the Lord for wonderful friends in Christ. They overlook the clutter and dust of our lives. They see us and our surroundings as works in progress. They recognize the potential for beauty on the horizon. By their encouragement, they spur us on to finish the job. Our best friends realize we all, in Christ, are at the "genesis" of a greater and grander future.

Prayer: Help me, Lord, to remember that those whose lives are "out of order" have the greatest need for friends; in Jesus' name. Amen

A Heart Made Fit for Friendship

Anger is cruel, and wrath is like a flood, but jealousy is even more dangerous. ~ Proverbs 27:4 (NLT)

Growing up, we did everything together – elementary school, Sunday school, church, Brownies. We biked and skated together, bowled and baked cookies together. Whatever we did, we did together. But our hearts remained out of sync because mine felt a nagging envy.

Judy always seemed to be two steps ahead of me. She watched late-night TV but I still went to bed at nine. She drank soda, but I still drank milk. She and her head full of bouncy, blond curls, drove me nuts! And the "straw that broke the camel's back?" Our Girl Scout leader, when assigning roles for an annual stage production, gave Judy the role of "Sleeping Beauty" and decided I should play *her father, the king*!

College separated us, but during those years I turned my heart to God. Confessing my sin, I realized the envy hadn't originated in the abundance of Judy's blessings, but from my failure to recognize and appreciate my own.

Today, Judy and I live miles apart but what we share is more valuable than everyday childhood activities. We both love the Lord and love discussing his Word. We share prayer concerns. My envy long gone, my heart is filled with joy that Judy is my friend.

Envy will crowd out the blessings. We must not let that happen.

Christmas 2008
(Letter)

Dear Family and Friends,

It has been quite a year, and like us you might be worried about all the cracks in your 401k retirement nest egg (now a "201k"). So we decided to write a Christmas letter of personal vignettes—happenings in 2008 that made us smile. Hope our stories do the same for you.

It's All Relative ~ We learned "it's all relative" when we sold our NJ home (June '07) and lived the next 15 months in the mountains. Lake Pleasant, NY is a small Adirondack village with a few, large and prominent families.

We soon discovered that the man who plowed our driveway was son-in-law to our electrician, whose daughters owned a sandwich shop in town and whose wife led the community chorus.

The house painter's sister was the former mayor. They were two of eight siblings and we ran into one of them wherever we went. One of the mayor's sisters sold us our kitchen appliances at a furniture store about an hour away. She's not only a great salesperson, she sings with the community chorus—the one conducted by the electrician's wife, who halfway through the concert lays down her conductor's baton, picks up her flute, and joins the community band. (We could go on and on, but by now you get the idea.)

It took John and me a little while to figure out who was related to whom. We almost attended the funeral of someone we didn't know, because he had the identical name as his cousin. Reminded us of the three brothers named Darrell on the old *Bob Newhart Show*.

Let it Snow! Let it Snow! Let it Snow! ~ Tons of the white stuff came down! 140" to be exact. And every Sunday, a certain member at North Country Bible Church requested prayer for more—a "first" in our church-going experience. The local economy rose and fell with the barometer, so week after week we honored his request for prayer and our lavish Lord honored those prayers in abundance. Often we'd hear TV meteorologists report, "Today's snow in the Adirondacks is tapering off—except at Lake Pleasant." Snowmobiles (a.k.a. snow machines—thank you, Sarah Palin!) tracked into town in record numbers. Drivers reported, "There's no snow anyplace else, not even in the heart of Buffalo."

Our driveway had to be plowed several times a week (sometimes several times a day), and grew increasingly more narrow. Finally a front end loader had to be brought in to haul it all away. Be assured, the local businesses did well!

Sinatra Can Still Melt a Man's Heart ~ The owner of The Inn at Speculator has a fine voice and occasionally entertains diners by singing with his karaoke machine. We were there Valentine's Day and he crooned one romantic song after the next. Six burly men in their mid-60s shared a table nearby. Dressed in rough flannel shirts, and coveralls, they'd been snowmobiling all afternoon.

They enjoyed a few beers with their dinner and seemed to know all the lyrics. They requested one Sinatra tune after the next and getting into the spirit of the innkeeper's repertoire, even sang along. He delighted in having so appreciative an audience and we enjoyed watching the performer-audience interaction. So busy singing love songs, they seemed to forget their wives were at home – alone on Valentine's Day!

Voter High-Jinx ~ Hamilton County is Republican; the only county in NYS that didn't go to Hillary when she ran for Senate. While casting my Primary Day ballot, I overheard John chatting with the poll worker. J: "How many registered voters here?" PW: "601." J: "How many Democrats?" PW: "126." J: "Are you nice to them?" PW: "Sure. Sometimes we even let them vote twice."

Have I Reached the Party to Whom I am Speaking? ~ Summer brought many visitors this year, starting in June when long-time friends came from Iowa and downstate NY. Knowing we expected three of them, they tried to telephone us when a fourth family member was able to get time off and come along. Not only did they wish to revise the headcount, they were now coming from NYC, not Albany, and had to revise their time of arrival.

They called repeatedly for three days but never connected with us. We discovered later that they had been dialing the wrong area code. They had left their messages on the answering machine of a stranger in the Midwest, messages like: "We are coming." "We are bringing an extra person." "We're coming from New York and look forward to being with you." "We'll stay three nights." Someone suggested calling that same number after their visit with us and leaving one final message: "Thanks for your hospitality. We had a great time!"

Prayer Changes Things ~ A friend once advised "Pray. Then step out and trust God to bring your foot down in the right place. The raised foot, poised for one direction, can come down in quite another!" That's exactly what happened to us this year. After months of exploring communities in NY, we moved to PA! You couldn't be more surprised than we! And we couldn't be more delighted!

"A-town" is a proud place. It is the home of the Allentown Band, the nation's oldest civilian band. Nearby we have the world-renowned Bach Choir of Bethlehem. Bixler's is America's oldest jewelry store, and The Moravian Bookstore in Bethlehem is the world's oldest bookshop.

Several colleges are within minutes of home including Muhlenberg – named for the first Lutheran pastor in North America. DeSales University presents marvelous theatre, and there's even more! Beautiful Trexler Memorial Park is only two blocks from home. But best of all, we have Wegmans – the supermarket to beat all others, right across from our back yard. If our 201k holds out, we no longer have to cook.

Carpe Diem ~ When the Phillies were positioned to win the World Series, we joined the PA frenzy and purchased team caps and sweatshirts. The next day some die-hard Yankee-fan friends from New York stopped by to check out our new digs and demanded to know, "When did you switch allegiances?" We had not yet watched a game and told them, "Yesterday, at Dick's Sporting Goods Store!"

Drive-thru Flu Shots ~ We discovered that Pennsylvanians have unique ways of doing things. For instance, one Sunday afternoon this fall Lehigh Valley Hospital offered drive-thru flu shots. The inoculations were given free of charge because the "not for profit" hospital had made a profit! So we lined up with countless motorists, presented our completed website application, and answered "No" to a volunteer's "Any allergies to eggs or latex?" Then we handed a bag of can goods to a volunteer from the Allentown food pantry, and drove through the parking lot to what looked like a multi-lane turnpike toll plaza.

Instead of toll-booths, rows of tables held medical paraphernalia and we drove up to one of many that were "manned" by cheerful nurses. I removed my jacket and Ms Nurse jabbed my upper arm right through the open window. Now we understood why the website said not to have animals in the car! We saw entire families in some vehicles and four nurses "doing their thing" simultaneously through four open windows. Gave new meaning to a family's Sunday drive. Wish I had thought to bring a camera.

Another Church "First" ~ In all our combined years of church attendance, we had to come to Pennsylvania for another "first." Would you believe it? A Sunday morning fire drill (*after* the sermon)! We thought it very smart and wondered why we'd never experienced this before.

3,300 Years and Counting ~ One day a workman built a booth on our new next door neighbor's patio. I'd seen similar booths years ago in certain sections of the Bronx and John had seen this annual building of booths in Brooklyn. Somehow, seeing it right next door made a big impression! Our neighbor is Jewish and was preparing to celebrate the Old Testament Festival of Booths. Boggles the mind to think that Moses gave instructions for this observance over 3,300 years ago and it is still faithfully observed to this day. (Check it out. Read Leviticus 23:33-34; 42-43.)

Christmas at "The Villas at Trexler Park" ~ Every day our townhouse community grows more lovely with Christmas lights and decorations. Recently an overnight dusting of snow added to the charm.

Refreshing Times of Friendship

(We're happy to take our snow a dusting at a time, thank you. Pay loaders were meant for Lake Pleasant!)

When a friend visited I told her "This is the prettiest house I've ever lived in" and she responded, "This is the prettiest house I've ever seen!" So now, that's become our price of admission. When you cross our threshold, we expect to hear, "This is the prettiest house I've ever seen!" Practice saying that line and come visit when it's convenient. Just telephone first and if you leave a message, make sure you've dialed the right area code.

***

May your Christmas be filled with joy! And may you be blessed with health and happiness in the year ahead. Let's all remember to pray for our nation and for our nation's leaders.

Love,
Helene and John

Billowing Clouds of Witness

Distinguished

Then Moses said to him, "If your Presence does not go with us, do not send us up from here. How will anyone know that you are pleased with me and with your people unless you go with us? What else will distinguish me and your people from all the other people on the face of the earth?" ~ Exodus 33:15-16 (NIV)

I held various positions during my career in the oil industry, but the assignment I remember most fondly is the one for which I had no preparation. My predecessor had retired and there was no one available to train me. I was on my own, but the new job didn't seem complicated. I primarily had to pay highway use taxes, and register all the company's Northeast Region trucks – tank trucks, tractor-trailers, package vehicles, pick-ups, etc.

I figured out my responsibilities from the mail that arrived at my desk each day – letters, forms, documents, applications. I literally learned by the "in-basket technique." Daily I asked the Lord to be with me on the job, and I felt his presence. The first few weeks went well.

Then, in early December, a policeman came to the office looking for me; I nearly died! The County Supervisor had sent him because the New York Department of Motor Vehicles had not received the company's 300-plus registration renewals. She wanted to remind me that they would all expire midnight, December 31. *Remind me? This was my first notice!*

I envisioned the fleet idle for lack of plates on New Year's Day and worked feverishly to process the 300 renewals. The new registration cards and license plates arrived back at my desk on Dec. 23, but the project wasn't over. I still needed to sort and distribute them to eight terminals throughout the state.

Staying late Christmas Eve, I spread 500 license plates on the floor of a long hallway and matched them up with windshield stickers and registration cards – by 17-digit VIN (vehicle identification number)! Then, after determining each truck's "home base," I packaged everything for UPS delivery. Garage foremen had just a week to change the plates as the trucks came into each shop. Whew!

The Lord had been with me on that job, but I didn't tell anyone that. Then one day, a co-worker, who'd once been a truck driver, surprised me with a question. "You don't cuss, Helene, do you?" he asked. Well, what do you know! The Lord had been with me, but not just to help me succeed, or to keep the company's "rolling stock" rolling; his purpose was bigger than that. "His presence was with me," and because I didn't cuss, even under pressure, I was "distinguished from others" around me. What a great opening I now had to share my faith!

Prayer: Lord, be with us on our jobs. May your presence be what distinguishes us. Be near, Lord Jesus.

2 Peter 1:5-9 (GW)

Because of this, make every effort to add integrity to your faith; and to integrity add knowledge; to knowledge add self-control; to self-control add endurance; to endurance add godliness; to godliness add Christian affection; and to Christian affection add love. If you have these qualities and they are increasing, it demonstrates that your knowledge about our Lord Jesus Christ is living and productive. If these qualities aren't present in your life, you're shortsighted and have forgotten that you were cleansed from your past sins.

Tracks in the Snow

He must also have a good reputation with outsiders, so that he will not fall into disgrace and into the devil's trap. ~ 1 Timothy 3:7 (NIV)

Walking up our driveway after retrieving the mail, I noticed the most unusual tracks in the snow. My husband stood in the doorway and I pointed them out to him.

"What in the world kind of animal left these tracks?" I asked and John stepped out for a closer look. We could easily recognize squirrel and deer prints, but the loopy shape of the new tracks baffled us.

I went into the house, removed my snowy jacket and then noticed that my new boots were leaving wet imprints on the kitchen floor – not of the whole shoe but just the middle part of the sole. There they were again, the same unidentifiable tracks. What a laugh! The strange animal that had left prints in the driveway was me!

As we travel through life we leave impressions. Oftentimes we are oblivious to the affect our behavior has on others, but still we leave an imprint – for good or for ill. How wonderful it is when others can identify the Lord's influence on our lives by the tracks we leave.

Prayer: Lord God, I know I've offended others and haven't always left a good impression. I need your help to do better; in Jesus' name. Amen

Matthew 11:2-5 (NLT)

John the Baptist, who was in prison, heard about all the things the Messiah was doing. So he sent his disciples to ask Jesus, "Are you the Messiah we've been expecting, or should we keep looking for someone else?"

Jesus told them, "Go back to John and tell him what you have heard and seen – the blind see, the lame walk, those with leprosy are cured, the deaf hear, the dead are raised to life, and the Good News is being preached to the poor."

Show or Tell

...I will show you my faith by the good things I do. ~ James 2:18 (GW)

Anna Pavlova (1881-1931) studied at the Imperial Ballet School in St. Petersburg, Russia and joined the Imperial Ballet in 1899. A brilliant star in the world of dance, she wowed audiences around the world. Her work has influenced the art form even to this day.

On one occasion, a member of the audience had the opportunity to meet Pavlova after a strenuous performance. He asked her, "Can you tell me what the dance meant? What was the story told by your dance?" Still perspiring from being on stage, she replied, "If I could put the story into words, I wouldn't have had to dance it."

Similarly, I feel the same frustration when I try to explain all that the Lord means to me. I cannot encapsulate in words, the depth and breadth of God's love. By his grace, I must simply endeavor to live it.

Prayer: Lord God, your word tells us you created the music of the spheres. May the dance of my life demonstrate your love daily; in Jesus' name. Amen

To the Jungles!

This command I'm giving you today isn't too hard for you or beyond your reach. It's not in heaven. You don't have to ask, "Who will go to heaven to get this command for us so that we can hear it and obey it?" This command isn't on the other side of the sea. You don't have to ask, "Who will cross the sea to get it for us so that we can hear it and obey it?" No, these words are very near you. They're in your mouth and in your heart so that you will obey them. ~ Deuteronomy 30:11-14 (GW)

The church of my childhood recruited many young people to work in foreign missions. Our pastor often heaped praises on all who took the challenge. But I, being young, misinterpreted his comments – and the nature of God. I mistakenly thought I'd be sent to some faraway and mysterious land if I fully committed my life to Christ. Specifically, I feared I'd be asked to travel to the jungles of deepest Africa. I did not want to go. I could not leave my home and family! No, I couldn't – and wouldn't – let God take full command of my life.

As an adult my thinking matured. I remember one day complimenting a friend for becoming a missionary to Borneo. I told her how I admired her greatly for all she was sacrificing to serve the Lord. She astounded me when she objected. "I'm not giving anything up," she said. "I love to go camping! This is what I love to do!"

Then it dawned on me! God is so big and so loving, he meets us where we are. He created each of us with unique personalities and interests; he knows and understands us. And he has work for each of us to do. Furthermore, he does not send every single one of his children to Africa!

I know today, that whatever the Lord asks us to do, he will also enable us to complete it. Jesus is Immanuel, "God with us," and we are strengthened by his presence in whatever work he has for us to do.

Prayer: Dear Lord, you are all-powerful yet you are gracious to me. You know my fears and limitations and you lend me your strength and courage. I want to serve you Lord; give me work we can accomplish together. Be with me for it is in your name, Immanuel, that I pray. Amen

A City on a Hill

"You are light for the world. A city cannot be hidden when it is located on a hill." ~ Matthew 5:14 (GW)

Why do we hesitate to share our faith with others? I couldn't put my finger on the reason last Sunday when our pastor posed the question in his sermon.

The usual reasons – or perhaps excuses – came to my mind: fear of rejection, fear of making a mistake, fear of looking foolish, fear of not knowing enough scripture. But as I gave it more thought, I hit upon this idea: Could it be that we intuitively know there may be a price to pay?

Every six months my church collects cans of yams to donate to the city's food pantry. *Are the yams to be donated in the name of Christ?* I wondered. *Do we put our church name or the name of Jesus on the cans that we give?*

The food company affixes its label and everyone is okay with that. No one complains that the company is bragging or trying to reach more customers. And many Christian organizations advertise their names when they perform works of charity. They like to point to Jesus as the one who taught us to share with those in need. Yet many of us on the local level are afraid. If we added a church label (something like "Shared with you by the members of First Church"), we fear other people in the community would not like it.

Our church's business card contains the motto: "God's work. Our hands." Perhaps even that affixed to the cans of yams would be a way to start becoming "a city on a hill."

Wouldn't our Heavenly Father be pleased to see us venture out and take even this first step?

Anna and Ina

...and she [Anna, a prophet] had been a widow for 84 years. Anna never left the temple courtyard but worshipped day and night by fasting and praying. ~ Luke 2:37 (GW)

Don't you know that your body is a temple that belongs to the Holy Spirit? The Holy Spirit, whom you received from God, lives in you. You don't belong to yourselves. ~ 1 Corinthians 6:19 (GW)

Ina had once worked on foreign mission fields, but age now confined her to a "seniors" apartment. Though in her nineties, her zeal for the Lord remained undiminished; she witnessed daily to the other residents in her building.

When I visited her one afternoon, she told me, "I'm frail. I no longer can go into the world. But the Lord is bringing the world to me."

How true! Ina's home-health caregivers came from all nations and ethnicities. "Most do not speak English, but I share the Gospel with them all," she said.

"What about the language barrier?" I questioned.

"Well, Honey," she said, "first I love them. Then they start to notice that I'm different from their other clients. I consider their needs, not just my own. After a while, they find a way to ask me why I'm happy in spite of my being homebound and weak. That's when I tell them I know the Lord."

Just like Anna the Prophetess, Ina never "left the temple." The presence of God traveled with her throughout life.

Prayer; Lord, may we never "leave the temple," the place of your presence, or retire from the job you have for us to do; in Jesus' name. Amen

Multiplying the Light[xviii]

"You are the light of the world. A city on a hill cannot be hidden. Neither do people light a lamp and put it under a bowl. Instead they put it on its stand, and it gives light to everyone in the house. In the same way, let your light shine before men, that they may see your good deeds and praise your Father in heaven." ~ Matthew 5:14-16 (NIV)

You are my lamp, O LORD; the LORD turns my darkness into light.
~ 2 Samuel 22:29 (NIV)

Hurricane Floyd knocked out the electricity and plunged my husband and me into darkness. We grabbed a flashlight and found the candles and matches in a kitchen drawer. Soon we had enough light to play checkers by – and to reminisce the evening away.

The storm raging outside brought back memories of past storms when the lights went out. I remembered that my mother placed lit candles in front of the dining room mirror, thus doubling the amount of illumination in the room.

This puzzled me as a child. How could a mere reflection provide additional light? The candles in the mirror were not real! How could something that wasn't "real" do anything? Yet the room was brighter; there was no denying that. The moon doesn't generate its own light either but reflects light to the earth from the sun.

It's similar with God's children. We cannot generate our own goodness. We can only reflect the goodness of the Lord as we allow his love to shine on us.

Prayer: Lord God, shine your heavenly goodness on me, that I might share the Good News of salvation in Christ with the world, especially in stormy weather; in Jesus' name. Amen

Waterfalls of God's Love

Stereotypes

...they asked his disciples: "Why does he eat with tax collectors and sinners?" ~ Mark 2:16 (GW)

When my husband and I vacationed in the mountains and had breakfast at a small diner, a rugged-looking guy came in. He wore jeans and a flannel shirt and took a stool at the counter. We noticed him because he was so warmly greeted by everyone – a well-liked, popular fellow.

We asked our server about him and learned that he was the town's tax assessor. Later, when we left the diner we discovered his pick-up truck parked outside. His license plate boldly advertised: TAX MAN. We thought this amazing. How can anyone love a tax man?

How different was the public opinion of Matthew, the tax collector described in the Bible. He was corrupt and greedy. Everyone hated him. The community wondered that Jesus didn't seem to recognize that. Why did he choose to welcome Matthew, and even dine with him? The community, feeling superior, was scandalized!

The crowd did not understand that if Jesus didn't associate with Matthew, he wouldn't associate with any of us. And without him, we are all lost. Jesus draws us to himself, brings us to repentance, and enables us to live honest lives. He gives us the same opportunity he gave Matthew. Popular opinion may stereotype certain professions, but Jesus looks into and changes our individual hearts.

Prayer: Heavenly Father, we admit we sometimes feel superior to others. Help us to put aside baseless prejudices. We know that your touch changes lives; in Jesus' name. Amen

The Unveiling

As all of us reflect the Lord's glory with faces that are not covered with veils, we are being changed into his image with ever-increasing glory. This comes from the Lord, who is the Spirit. ~ 2 Corinthians 3:18 (GW)

I caught my sister Thyra studying the calendar on the wall. Another of her milestone birthdays was approaching and she seemed melancholy. She is the oldest of my siblings but she has more energy, interests, and activities than just about everyone I know – regardless of age. She is not old, but nevertheless as her special day approached, she started to feel ancient.

I decided the family needed to help her face the new decade; to show her how youthful she is in our eyes. So I visited a chalk artist's cart at the local mall and arranged for him to draw her portrait. He was impressed when he looked over the photo I'd handed him. "Very good-looking woman," he remarked and then added, "I'll take out some of her wrinkles."

"Wonderful," I said. He'd obviously understood my intentions. I couldn't have been happier as he wrote up the order. I felt confident that the surprise portrait would lift my sister's spirits. She would see herself as the vibrant person we know her to be. I'm sure the Lord sees her that way also. For in spite of all our shortcomings and failings, he always sees beauty worth rescuing.

Our Creator God is the portraitist beyond compare, for he doesn't simply work on the surface appearance. He comes into our lives and transforms us in the secret places of our hearts. He works his artistry from the inside out and we develop a new beauty as we reflect his goodness and love. It's an on-going process, one that has nothing to do with birthdays.

Prayer: Creator God, come into my life and transform me. You alone, through Christ, can remove the "wrinkles" of sin. Change me day by day, year by year, from the inside out, until the outside reflects the beauty of your goodness and love.

John 1:46-50 (GW)

Nathanael said to Philip, "Can anything good come from Nazareth?"

Philip told him, "Come and see!"

Jesus saw Nathanael coming toward him and remarked, "Here is a true Israelite who is sincere."

Nathanael asked Jesus, "How do you know anything about me?"

Jesus answered him, "I saw you under the fig tree before Philip called you."

Nathanael said to Jesus, "Rabbi, you are the Son of God! You are the king of Israel!"

Jesus replied, "You believe because I told you that I saw you under the fig tree. You shall see greater things than that."

See for Yourself

"Nazareth!" exclaimed Nathanael. "Can anything good come from Nazareth?" "Come and see for yourself," Philip replied. ~ John 1:46 (NLT)

My sister Dorothy, a teenage fan of a certain rock star, bought all his recordings and saw all his movies. When he performed live in New York City, she caught the matinee performance and later spoke of her experience to the family over dinner.

She described an elaborate pre-show act to "warm up" the audience. It continued for over an hour. The pumped-up audience grew impatient. When the singer was finally announced, the spotlights glared, drums thumped, pulsing electric guitars screeched to a frightening pitch, and the audience screamed and jumped up from their seats. The star, elaborately costumed and appearing larger-than-life, bounded onto the stage. Some teens near my sister were in tears, so great their frenzy.

Our father asked her, "What did you think about all this?"

Dorothy said she still liked the singer but it seemed as if many were there, not to enjoy his talent, but to worship him as an idol.

I find it interesting that Philip in today's reading, did not provide any "advance hype" or try to affect Nathanael's perception of Jesus. Philip seemed to understand that Jesus wants people to see him for who he is. Furthermore, when we allow Jesus to see us for who we really are, he is able to touch our hearts with his love and mercy.

Prayer: Lord Jesus, it's me, coming to you just as I am. I need to know you for myself. Come into my life and bless me. Amen

To Curry Favor

In the council of the holy ones God is greatly feared; he is more awesome than all who surround him. ~ Psalm 89:7 (NIV)

I told my friend Helga that I planned to write to an opera star in Europe and she said, "You can't write a fan letter just like that." She held her hand high over her head. "He's up there," she said. "And you're down here," she continued, bringing her hand to knee level.

"That's ridiculous," I said. But she responded, "You Americans don't know any better."

Now she had my attention. She was born overseas. What did I know of European propriety?

So I listened as she cautioned that there was a right way and a wrong way to approach important people. She said I shouldn't write in English. She would translate, using the finest grammar and the most polite language. In the opening sentence we would apologize for writing!

Her comments and suggestions depressed me. My genuine exuberance over the singer's fine performance on American TV and my desire to write and congratulate him soon got lost in a fog of flowery flattery. I gave up the project.

Sometime later, I decided to try again, this time without Helga's help. I simply wrote from my heart and the letter paved the way to some surprising events. I got to shake his hand, discovered he was gracious and appreciative. He even stood with my sisters and me for a picture.

I think of that experience whenever I consider the greatness of God. In terms of power and might, glory and perfection, holiness and love, he truly is way "up there" and we truly are way "down here." But through Jesus Christ we may go to God directly, not with flowery flattery but with a humble heart full of genuine praise. How ironic that a feeling of unworthiness should cause us to hesitate and hold back from approaching, when all the time his arms are outstretched to welcome, forgive, comfort, and embrace us – just as we are.

Prayer: Heavenly Father, your arms are outstretched and you say "Come unto me." Help me to run to your embrace without hesitation; in Jesus' name. Amen

Luke 2:8-10 (GW)

Shepherds were in the fields near Bethlehem. They were taking turns watching their flock during the night. An angel from the Lord suddenly appeared to them. The glory of the Lord filled the area with light, and they were terrified. The angel said to them, "Don't be afraid! I have good news for you, a message that will fill everyone with joy."

No Angels, Please

As a father has compassion on his children, so the LORD has compassion on those who fear him; for he knows how we are formed, he remembers that we are dust. ~ Psalm 103:13-14 (NIV)

My sister Dorothy's last days were difficult and after her death I felt empty. The Lord – directly and through family and friends – surrounded me with love and help, but I could not find peace.

One night as I prayed, I recalled the many accounts I'd recently read of God sending angels to minister to the suffering and sorrowful. "O, Lord," I prayed, "I want your peace but please do not send me an angel. If I awake in the middle of the night and there is a heavenly being at the foot of my bed, I couldn't take it. I'm so tired, so shaken."

Just as many people in the Bible experienced terror at the appearance of angelic beings, I too was afraid. I could not bear to be in the presence of such heavenly holiness.

I fell asleep with this strange prayer on my lips: "…no angels….". I awoke the next day without receiving peace. But a few days later an unexpected package arrived at my front door. I opened it with apprehension, not knowing what I'd find. Inside the box, staring up at me, was an angel my friend Karen had crocheted over an old soda bottle. It had a wooly, white robe and a golden crown. It was beautiful and I wept.

God had had his way, sent me an "angel" from a caring friend. And it brought a good measure of that peace which is beyond understanding.

Prayer: Heavenly Father, forgive us when we try to "second guess" how you might answer our prayers. Help us to remember that you take our human frailties into account and supply our needs with grace and mercy; in Jesus' name. Amen

Unclassified[xix]

There is neither Jew nor Greek, slave nor free, male nor female, for you are all one in Christ Jesus. ~ Galatians 3:28 (NIV)

I have my race, nationality, social standing, economic class, gender, education, marital status, and income level. I'm sure the pollsters think they know my political leanings and the marketers have me pegged to buy certain products. The supermarkets issue me coupons they've tailored to my past buying habits, and the telemarketers associate my giving with certain charities. Everybody thinks they have me figured out. They think they know me, because they have pigeon-holed me one way or another.

Only God knows the inmost secrets of my being, who I really am. And that's not based on any external trappings of the groups to which I belong. He knows me. He loves me. He welcomes me through the sacrifice of his Son, Jesus. He sees past the externals and looks into my heart.

I pray that he would give me that same ability in my dealings with others.

The Best Heart-Shaped Greeting in the World[xx]
(Fiction Short Story)

It was a Friday afternoon in May, and the sun shone brightly in the classroom window. This was the day spring fever should have made its debut to make lively third graders long for roller skates and ice cream and fidget for the three o'clock bell. This special day, the Friday before Mother's Day, thirty pairs of pudgy hands worked feverishly on their choice of greeting cards or crepe paper roses.

Miss Nelson studied her charges, but her thoughts kept returning to Beth, whose bright red head bobbed with enthusiasm as tiny fingers cut, glued, printed, and crayoned. So intent on her project, nothing mattered but to create the best heart-shaped greeting in the world.

Beth's mother had not visited since Christmas, and everything had to be right for the occasion. Though her foster parents were kind, they were older and could have passed for grandparents. They did not satisfy the intense longing for a "real" mother, especially for Beth's young and glamorous mom.

Beth glowed with anticipation as she poured excitement and joy into her creation. She made the biggest red heart she could, then fastened it to a large, lacy doily. She tied a bow and glued it to the top and hung shiny ribbons from the bottom. In the center, she crayoned two bluebirds. They were chirping quarter notes like those the music teacher always drew.

When Miss Nelson suggested a second card for her Nana, Beth rested her sticky hands, sat back and wrestled with the idea. "No. I'd rather not," she said. "Sunday is for my 'real' mom."

When the big day finally came, Beth was ready. She had bathed the night before with jasmine bubble bath and polished her Sunday pumps twice to a gleaming shine. With great care, she dressed in her navy blue skirt and the blouse with the wide sailor collar. Nana managed to fix a white ribbon in her short hair. Even though she was two hours early,

Beth made a final check in the foyer mirror and seated herself on the front steps to wait. She fingered the most beautiful card in the world. Inside, Nana set the table for three o'clock coffee and prayed, "Dear Lord, please make her show up this time. Let Beth have her 'real' mother today."

Classmates came by and called her to play, but Beth would not leave her post; she had begun her long vigil. When she tired of sitting, she walked the length of the porch. She sat. She paced. She waited. As the day dragged on, the sky filled with clouds and by five, a fine mist started to fall. When the hall clock struck six, she left her card on the step and ran to the old neighbor next door.

"Mr. Tully, may I cut a rose?" she asked. "It's for my mother." Tully raised a woolly brow. "Did she come?" he inquired. Beth lowered her gaze. She was not accustomed to lying. "Yes," came a timid reply. Then gaining courage and enjoying the sound of the false words she added glibly, "She's been here hours already."

He gave the pale child a rose. Grabbing the flower, she ran home in a downpour, took the front steps two at a time, and let the front door bang behind her. Beth's clothes were drenched and dirty, but when Nana heard the noise she rushed down the stairs and there in the hallway, they fell into each other arms. Sobbing, she clung to Nana's embrace and endless tears began their flow.

"Here," she said, thrusting out her hand, "not like the fake roses made in school. This is real. I love you, Nana." Outside in the storm, the rain pounded the best heart-shaped greeting in the world.

Morningstar, Direction of the Family

My Dad's Christmas[xxi]

Wise words are more valuable than much gold and many rubies.
~ Proverbs 20:15 (NLT)

Mom snapped a photo on Christmas morning many years ago, and it has become our family's all-time favorite. My dad is playing his violin, my oldest sister is seated at the piano, and my two other sisters and I are singing *Away in a Manger*. We are gathered around my grandfather's old upright, the one we inherited along with his house when he died suddenly two years earlier.

My parents, busy with work and rearing their four daughters, had not yet made changes to the living room's decor, so the furnishings captured in the picture reflect the style of my grandparents' day. An Oriental rug covers the hardwood floor with a colorful pattern of flora and fauna. Crocheted coverings protect the arms of the red velvet loveseat. Near the piano, to throw extra light on the sheet music, stands a floor lamp with hexagonal shade, and above the piano hangs a framed canvas depicting a Victorian courting scene.

The painting fascinated me, even at five years of age. A young man, seated on a park bench, glances longingly at a demure young lady. He shares the bench, not with his beloved, but with her chaperoning parents. The mother is intent on engaging the young man in conversation, and the father is patiently sitting with his hands extended and wrapped with yarn as his daughter, seated across from him, winds the wool into a large ball.

The painting evokes a number of stories, featuring the love-struck fellow, the woman who shyly holds his attention, and the chatty mother. But the most striking message for me concerns the father. Sitting quietly, he's just there, unobtrusively watching out for the welfare of his daughter just as my dad would now do for his four girls on that Christmas morning.

Like most children, I'd gone to bed the night before all pumped up with anticipation for Santa's visit and the wonderful gifts I hoped he would leave. When morning came, my sisters and I charged down the stairs to find a glistening tree with a number of intriguing packages waiting for us. We were "hopped up" and eager to explore and possess, but my dad called a halt to our rush.

"Let's keep everything in perspective," he said, glancing at the gifts before turning his attention back to us. "Christmas is about the birth of Jesus. Before we do anything else, let's sing a few carols."

Mom agreed and sent us upstairs to dress for church. Dad readied his violin bow with rosin and when we returned, Thyra took her seat on the piano bench. Dorothy, Marilyn and I, now dressed in our Sunday best, stood and sang. In that moment, my mother snapped the treasured photo.

I cannot remember what marvelous items we found wrapped under the tree that morning. Whatever they were, I'm sure they were wonderful and made us happy. They have long since perished. One gift, however, has lasted – the memory of my dad keeping Christ in Christmas.

The longer I live, the more evidence I see that the riches of this world do not last. What counts most are the unseen riches of love, peace, harmony, a good name and reputation, the fellowship of faithful friends, and the ties of a loving family. And even greater than these, is the blessing God gives when he brings people into our lives who will point us to Christ and, with great wisdom, show us the way to salvation.

Mom[xxii]

Direct your children onto the right path, and when they are older, they will not leave it. ~ Proverbs 22:6 (NLT)

Helen wanted to sing like all her classmates. She just couldn't seem to match the tones and she dreaded the music teacher who came to her grammar school every week. The teacher would have the class stand in chorus formation, sound her pitch pipe, and wave her arms. But it wasn't long before she'd drop them again.

"Hold everything," she'd say. "Let me hear the boys." Only the boys would sing.

"Okay. Now only the girls." And the girls sang.

She'd narrow her focus on a small group of singers and finally work her way down a specific row. My mother, the non-singer, knew she'd soon be found out.

The rest of the class remained silent as the teacher hit one key on the piano after the next, insisting my mother match the tones. Mom dropped her head and her voice diminished to a whisper. She tried. Her sweet face would turn red, and her blue eyes puff up with the tears she held back. The other children would giggle but the music teacher grew fierce in her determination. She would spend the remaining hour on her humiliating and fruitless efforts to teach this one student to carry a tune. Finally the school bell would ring and the class was dismissed.

Week after week, it was always the same torture for little Helen. Things would be different today, but in the early 1900s, when you were the child of hard-working, reserved European-born parents, you simply obeyed your teachers even when it meant suffering in silence.

Eventually, as Shakespeare would say, "Time and the hour runneth through the roughest of days." Mom graduated and moved on to high school, to work, to romance and marriage. She gave birth to four children – all daughters. I am one of those daughters and I know my mom never recovered from the treatment she received in grammar school music class.

She excelled in everything a mom should excel in, caring for her family, providing a wonderful and safe environment for her children. She could sew, she could cook, she could decorate birthday cakes and, because she loved music so much, she encouraged us to practice our piano lessons. Most importantly, she taught us about the Lord and brought us to Sunday school.

The only opportunity my mother had to sing as an adult was in church, but she didn't. She'd stand with the hymnbook open and read the words silently while everyone else sang out with confidence. Mom's "praise to the Lord" was her faithfulness as a wife and mother, homemaker, and friend. In church, when the organ swelled with majestic hymns and everyone sang as if consumed by the music, her lips remained closed.

Perhaps the greatest irony of my mother's life was that all four of her daughters grew up to become church organists and choir directors, and two – her eldest and youngest – became elementary school music teachers.

Dad[xxiii]

Train up a child in the way he should go: and when he is old, he will not depart from it. ~ Proverbs 22:6 (KJV)

A New York City Police Department patrolman by vocation, Dad was a musician by avocation. He'd grown up in an era when every child of German-immigrant parents had to learn to play a musical instrument. He was a young boy when his folks gave him his own violin. And it was expensive enough to span the gift budget of several Christmases. Every year, his parents took the violin out of its case and placed it, once again, under the Christmas tree. Even so Dad loved it, and all through his life spoke fondly of his treasured "Heberlein" and of his violin teacher, Mr. Klotz.

One day soon after he joined the police department in 1929, my father's vocation and avocation came together. Dad had just walked into the police station and he was greeted by his boss. "Hey, Fred," the sergeant said, putting his hand on Dad's shoulder, "you play the fiddle, don't you?" Dad nodded, and the sergeant continued. "Eugene LaBarre – he's the band director – needs someone who reads music to play the bass drum. He said he'd teach you how to drum if you're willing."

Willing? Believe me, Dad didn't need any encouragement. LaBarre was a civilian member of the force, but the police academy gave him the rank of captain because his credentials were so outstanding. Most notably, he had been a trumpeter in John Philip Sousa's band.

The Captain liked my father right away. He introduced him to the retiring drummer, Louis Wagenblast, who took him under his wing, and taught him how to hold the sticks and play drum rolls and paradiddles. All Dad needed to do was practice on the drum pad he brought home and practice he did! Every spare moment those sticks were tapping out various rhythms and routines.

Dad was in his glory beating that drum at rehearsals, marching in the city's big parades, and meeting the European dignitaries as their ships docked in New York Harbor. How he loved those official welcoming ceremonies. The band also made the rounds to the Veterans Administration hospitals and appeared at the opening of the George Washington Bridge (1931), and the Lincoln Tunnel (1937). They performed at the '39 World's Fair and gave concerts at Carnegie Hall.

Years later, when we kids were on the scene, we heard that muffled drum pad still being tapped all the time. At mealtime, Dad didn't bring his drum pad to the table, but he had his fingers and the kitchen table was sturdy Formica. While Mom put dinner on the table, Dad tapped his rolled digits with abandon. For laughs, my three sisters and I would take up the beat in fond imitation. I'm sure Dad was the most conscientious drummer a police band ever had.

Back then, New York City had three bands. The Police, the Fire, and the Sanitation Departments each had their own. All members were full-time employees of their respective services, and the band rehearsals were part of their tours of duty. So Dad was a policeman but had found his niche within the department.

How Dad enjoyed being in that band and participating in so many different venues and at so many special NYC events! The boys in the band were a busy bunch. Best part for the four Hollwegs daughters was that the band played on the radio.

Every Friday evening, WNYC would broadcast a live concert of one of the city's three bands. We loved it when it was the Police Department's turn. The school week was over; we had no homework that needed to be done that evening. The dinner dishes dried and put away, Mom would find WNYC on the old cabinet radio that took up a corner of our living room. We four sisters would form a queue and parade around the room to one Sousa march after the next.

What glee! We enjoyed every beat of the drum. We would not have been able to identify Dad so easily if he'd been one of the clarinetists or played the French horn, but any sound from the percussion section – drum, chimes, cymbals – was easy for us. "That's Dad!" we'd point to the radio and squeal with pride. How we loved marching around to his beat.

Dad was a policeman who loved his family, his home, and his music. He loved the pomp and dignity of New York's official occasions and he loved being in the middle of it all with his drum.

Just as when we were children and knew he was beating the drum – though he was miles away in the broadcasting studio – we can still hear the beat he set years ago when he encouraged my sisters and me in our music lessons and when he drove his four daughters to Sunday school every week. That early influence set the pace for us and the beat goes on.

Drummer Dad
(Essay)

When Dad joined the New York City Police Department Band, he practiced drumming technique every opportunity he had. It takes discipline and control to play percussion instruments well and he enjoyed the challenge. It suited his personality for he was a perfectionist. We saw that trait in everything he put his hand to. Around the house it was most evident in his home-owner repairs and handyman plumbing.

When he fixed a faucet, it stayed fixed. The only problem was that after he'd replaced a washer, no one else in the family had the strength required to turn the knob again. Mom said it required the muscles of Samson. She told us that Dad descended from a long-line of blacksmiths and simply never realized he was stronger than most people. Maddening for his progeny – four little girls!

His strength, however, was just what Captain LaBarre and the boys in the band needed. For parades he strapped the bass drum to his shoulders and carried it up Fifth Avenue riding on his broad chest. He didn't require a stand on wheels for his drum. He marched proudly and did what he could to make the entire band stand tall. Few things frustrated him more than sloppy marching. So, he beat the drum vigorously and never missed the count. His confident, commanding stroke kept the other sixty-four players in step and looking smart.

Although Dad's tour of duty involved paid band rehearsals, it also included the normal police work of "walking the beat." He loved being a patrolman when it meant getting to know the residents of a community or being of service. He'd tap the visor of his cap with the nightstick as he greeted passersby with a hearty "Ev'ning." He gave directions to out-of-towners, found children who were lost, helped those who'd locked themselves out of their cars or homes, and assisted the elderly or infirmed across the street. His greatest service to the community, however, was keeping the traffic moving at the wide Bronx intersection of Webster Avenue and Gun Hill Road, a street named for its historic past in the American Revolution.

Dad blew his whistle, and waved his arms with purpose and clarity, not unlike a symphony orchestra maestro conducting a spirited overture. His motions could have been set to music and in his head, probably were. Directing traffic is quite the cardio-vascular workout. It's no wonder that traffic cops and orchestra conductors live long lives.

As a child I worried that Dad's life might be cut short by all the cars whizzing by as he stood in the center of those two large avenues. I also worried he might have a heart attack waving his arms so rapidly, tooting that whistle and turning red in the face when some "dopey-diddle-dock" motorist failed to pay attention or react quickly enough when Dad motioned him on.

Daily his reputation grew. Motorists waiting in heavy, rush-hour traffic could tell a block or two away when "Fred" was on duty. How much they appreciated his efforts to keep that traffic flowing! Years after he had retired, new acquaintances would laugh with surprise when they recognized him. They'd say, "I know you. You're Fred the cop! Gun Hill and Webster!"

Early in his police career, Fred achieved real fame as attested to by the newspaper coverage. During the 1930s men in the junk, ice, or knife-sharpening businesses took their horse-drawn wagons up and down the streets of each city neighborhood. They jingled bells en route to gain the attention of housewife-customers. One day some youths, loitering along Fordham Road in the Bronx, saw a horse waiting quietly at the curb for the junkman to return from making a sale. They threw rocks at the animal and he bolted. He took off at breakneck speed and headed east with abandon, wagon in tow.

Fordham Road is a wide street, lined on both sides with many shoe stores and dress shops, movie theatres and, of course, the main campus of Fordham University. It was always heavy with motor and pedestrian traffic. A stressed out, and out-of-control animal, especially one so large as a horse pulling a junk wagon, can cause much damage to life and property. So, Dad commandeered a passing motorist, hopped on the running board, pointed, and shouted "Follow that horse!"

In those days, patrolmen did not cruise around the neighborhood in police cars. They walked the beat and private citizens knew that their cars and/or driving services were to be made available to the NYPD as emergencies might require. Just as today, we pull aside and stop for fire engines, when a policeman needed you or your car, you had no choice but to comply.

The stunned motorist gunned his gas pedal. With Dad on the running board, clinging to the car through the open passenger-side window, the two of them were off in a frantic chase across Fordham Road. The horse with swaying junk wagon in tow, and noisy pots and pans clanking, sped past terrified pedestrians and laughing school children. The cop and his commandeered motorist raced along in close pursuit. The winded junk man followed with arms flailing, trying to keep up on foot.

The horse ran through the majestic wrought iron gates of the Bronx Zoo and around the traffic circle immediately inside the entrance. The tall monkey cages were located nearby. What a commotion! Dad on the running board, chasing the horse and its noisy wagon round and round the circle, pigeons squawking and taking flight to avoid being trampled, and the monkeys joining the excitement hopping, swinging about, and squealing in their cages. At last, the horse tired out and slowed to a jog. The show ended without further incident and Dad led the exhausted animal, now compliant, back to its owner. "Keeping the peace" certainly has meant different things to different eras of police work. The mad chase across

Fordham Road was big news and given two columns in the evening papers.

Dad was also an excellent marksman and did well at his periodic reviews, but I don't believe he ever had to pull his pistol on the job – at least not at any people. He may have used his nightstick to tap the shoes of some "drunk" sleeping it off. But mainly his nightstick was used to tip his cap, or to swing and catch – a game he played with himself on lonely midnight shifts.

Aside from the junk wagon chase and an occasional response to the *Daily News*' Roving Reporter, Dad's photo made it into the newspapers every time the band paraded. He carried the biggest drum, the one whose drumhead advertised "Police Band City of New York." That's the shot the press photographers always sought out. That's the photo, in the entire newspaper, that my sisters and I loved the best.

Clothed in Her Love[xxiv]

Mom ran her Singer every day and often late into the night. I'd fall asleep listening to the motor's hum, the rhythmic clatter of needle and bobbin kissing. She'd produce one dress, skirt or jumper after the next – for herself and for my sisters and me. I don't know how she kept pace with four growing daughters.

Every Christmas and Easter all four of us received new outfits at the same time. How special to wear new clothes at our Sunday school programs! We looked nice, but Mom looked tired.

I remember vividly an outfit she made for me when I was five years old: a yellow print dress that sported a white scalloped collar. I stood on the stairway landing as she sat a few steps down and pinned the hem. Slowly I turned so she could check that it was even. She was particularly happy with how the collar turned out. "You look stylish, Helene," she said, "with the wide bib collar."

That did it! "Bibs are for babies!" I said and stomped away. She explained how everyone wore big collars, even showed me pictures in grown-up magazines of ladies wearing the latest styles. I would not be convinced.

She finished the dress but I don't remember ever wearing it. I guess I was, even then, sensitive to words. To me, wearing a "bib" was being a baby. I refused to do it.

Three years later I saw the dress again – crumpled on a shelf in the garage. Now one of my dad's rags, it was covered with grease. The beautiful little dress that Mom had made just for me and I had stubbornly refused to wear was now filthy and torn. In tears, I ran into the house and into my mother's arms. "I'm so sorry," I cried. "You made me that beautiful dress and I didn't appreciate it. You worked so hard on it and it was wonderful. I wish I could wear it now but it wouldn't fit!"

Full of remorse, I trembled and sobbed. Mom held me close, consoling me – not angry, not thinking of herself, her hard work, or her disappointment. I had treated her efforts shabbily. I didn't deserve her forgiveness, but she, ever a conduit of God's grace, comforted me, wrapped her arms around me, and clothed me in her love.

Saturday Morning Eggy-Peggy
(Essay)

When I was a child, growing up in the late 1940s and early '50s, I saw my father perform two Saturday-morning rituals every week without fail.

I'd wake up hearing the clanking of pots and bowls in the kitchen, telling me the first ritual was well in progress. Dad was preparing "Eggy-Peggy," something his mother created when he was a child to introduce him to soft-boiled eggs. It is simply bread and butter sandwiches, cut into cubes, mixed with the eggs, and salted to taste.

Hearing Dad play "chef," my three sisters and I raced each other to breakfast to claim the juicy bowl – the bowl in which he mixed this delicacy before he apportioned it out into the other three dry bowls. We loved this weekend treat, following five weekday mornings of Mom's hot oatmeal.

After we ate our fill, Dad began his second project. He took out the carton he'd gotten from a local shoe factory (about the size of four shoe boxes) and placed in it bags of flour, sugar, tea, coffee, paper goods, nylon hosiery, cigarettes, and insulin. Later he'd take it to the post office and mail it off to his elderly aunt in Germany, a diabetic whose provisions were scarce after the war. What she didn't consume herself, she shared with her neighbors or used as barter for other goods and services. It was a weekly ritual repeated by many Americans in those days – sending "care" packages to relatives living in a devastated Europe.

We watched with fascination how tightly Dad packed the contents. We laughed at the length of sticky tape and twine he wrapped round and round the box, but he boasted that every single shipment of his "got through" to its destination.

"Put your finger there," he'd say and point. He made me feel essential to the project as he secured a double knot with the strong cord.

My great aunt's appreciation knew no bounds. She wrote often to thank my dad and to list her needs as they changed. Even though her sight was failing, she once sent a "handkerchief" to show her appreciation. She embroidered it for my oldest sister from a piece of cheesecloth that had wrapped some food in one of Dad's earlier packages. The brand name stamped on the cloth was still visible and silently testified to the shortages in the country, and to Tante Etta's ingenious use of everything she had.

Today, when my sisters and I visit each other overnight, we sometimes, just for fun, make "Eggy-Peggy" for breakfast. And when we do, we thank the Lord for the abundance we enjoy in America, and for the wonderful memories of my father's generous spirit, his cheerful giving, and his faithfulness week after week, year after year.

~

Recipe

Make bread and butter sandwiches using rye bread. Cut them into cubes. Boil eggs for 1¾ - 2 minutes. (Use 1 egg per 2-3 slices of rye bread.) Scoop out the contents of each egg and mix in a bowl. Add salt to taste. Add the buttered bread cubes and mix together. Divide into individual portions. (Remember, the early riser gets to eat from the "juicy" bowl.)

Then, as my dad used to say, "Down the hatch!"

Dawn of the Holy Spirit

Recognizing Jesus[xxv]

The next day John saw Jesus coming toward him and said, "Look, the Lamb of God, who takes away the sin of the world!" ~ John 1:29 (NIV)

"Turn on the TV," my friend said over the phone. "Werner Hollweg is in an opera televised from Vienna!" I was so excited to hear this, I hung up without asking what part he was singing. I knew of this German tenor who had effectively the same family name as I; now I had the opportunity to see him. I flipped on Channel 13 immediately.

The opera *Ulysses* involved many mythical beings – Greek gods and goddesses, and various creatures of the sea. I studied the face of each character as it appeared, but the masks and heavy theatrical makeup made it impossible to distinguish facial features.

I watched for 20 frustrating minutes and was just about to telephone my friend, when the tenor who played the role of "Ulysses" appeared on stage. I couldn't believe it. It was as if I were looking at my father! The broad forehead, the full eyebrows, the chin, the cheek bones, the mouth – all matched my dad's. His nose was a different shape, but still the resemblance was striking. We just had to have some common ancestor, and I said aloud, "I'd know him anywhere!"

How did John the Baptist know Jesus when he saw him approach that day? Jesus was his second cousin but John didn't say, "This must be cousin Jesus. I'd recognize him anywhere." No, he said, "Look, the Lamb of God, who takes away the sin of the world." This surely was not an earthly experience of human kinship. It was an "inner knowing" of God, made possible by the Holy Spirit. (In Luke 1:15 KJV we read that John the Baptist was "filled with the Holy Ghost even from his mother's womb.")

Today, the same Holy Spirit who was in John comes to us through Scripture reading, prayer, and the sacraments. He makes Jesus, "the

Lamb of God who takes away the sin of the world," known to us and brings us into a right relationship with him.

Prayer: Heavenly Father, thank you that through the work of the Holy Spirit, we can know Jesus, distinguish him from all the mythical characters that clutter the stage of life. Draw us into a deeper relationship with him this Advent season; in his name we pray. Amen

***

Enlightened
(A 50-word or less devotion on a question Jesus asked)

Question: *Jesus asked him, "Do you believe this just because I told you I had seen you under the fig tree?"* … ~ John 1:50 (NLT)

Devotion: Jesus' invitation is always personal, intimate. He calls to my heart in ways tailor-made for me; other people might not understand. To Nathanael he said, "I saw you under the fig tree," and by those simple words, perhaps cryptic to others, captured forever the heart of his newest disciple.

The Comforter[xxvi]

And I will pray the Father, and he shall give you another Comforter, that he may abide with you for ever. ~ John 14:16 (KJV)

When I was a child, Dorothy Lungen taught me how to play the piano. And years later, when she was well into her eighties and still giving lessons, she taught a friend of mine, Cornelia. She was a senior citizen and beside studying piano, she volunteered countless hours each week at Rosary Hill Home (hospice care) in Hawthorne, NY.

One day Cornelia discovered that Miss Lungen enjoyed crocheting; so over the course of several years, she brought her a new supply of yarn every time she took a piano lesson. Dorothy Lungen, in her old age, sat alone in her apartment between Cornelia's visits, and crocheted granny-square afghans for the terminally ill residents of Rosary Hill. As she completed each, she'd give it to Cornelia, who in turn, brought it to the home. One of the Catholic sisters on staff there, wrote Miss Lungen a beautiful note of appreciation every single time.

When I read today's scripture verse, I think of Miss Lungen and all the marvelous, colorful, full-of-life-and-love comforters that she crocheted for those who were dying. Since the fall of mankind in the Garden of Eden, God has provided comfort to our dying race. But the Lord doesn't wrap us up in colorful yarn. He wraps us up, body and soul, in the Holy Spirit – the Comforter with a capital "C."

This Comforter never fades, never unravels, nor suffers the ravages of time. The Holy Spirit is the gift of God the Father, who brings us to life in Christ, and who will abide with us always.

Prayer: Thank you, Jesus, for praying to the Father to send us the Comforter – the Comforter who keeps us secure in the warm love of God, now and forever. Amen

Dorcas-Like

In Joppa there was a disciple named Tabitha (in Greek her name is Dorcas); she was always doing good and helping the poor. ~ Acts 9:36 (NIV)

"Dorcas, Miss Lungen, Cornelia" – the list goes on and on – but the list is not yet long enough.

Prayer: Lord, what would you have me do?

***

The Houseguest Who Never Leaves[xxvii]

Jesus replied, "If anyone loves me, he will obey my teaching. My Father will love him, and we will come to him and make our home with him." ~ John 14:23 (NIV)

Behold, I stand at the door, and knock: if any man hear my voice, and open the door, I will come in to him, and will sup with him, and he with me. ~ Revelation 3:20 (KJV)

My second cousin visited from Australia, and as we approached the end of her five-week stay, it became increasingly difficult to accomplish all that we wanted to do. We toured historic sites every day and chatted about family every evening. She taught me how to make scones and nectarine chutney, and she came with me to church and Bible study. Ours was a crash course in "getting to know you" – fun.

How nice it would be if she lived closer! We could get acquainted more gradually and avoid the pain of parting. In contrast, the Lord's presence in my life is ongoing. He doesn't have to leave to attend to the rest of his family. He abides with all who invite him to stay and remains with us for eternity.

Prayer: Lord God, how marvelous it is that you abide simultaneously with all your children worldwide. Stay near – now and forever; in Jesus' name. Amen

Deuteronomy 4:9-10 (GW)

However, be careful, and watch yourselves closely so that you don't forget the things which you have seen with your own eyes. Don't let them fade from your memory as long as you live. Teach them to your children and grandchildren. Never forget the day you stood in front of the LORD your God at Mount Horeb. The LORD had said to me, "Assemble the people in front of me, and I will let them hear my words. Then they will learn to fear me as long as they live on earth, and they will teach their children the same thing."

The Manager[xxviii]

For we know, brothers loved by God, that he has chosen you, because our gospel came to you not simply with words, but also with power, with the Holy Spirit and with deep conviction... ~ 1 Thessalonians 1:4-5 (NIV)

My boss offered me a promotion but insisted I first write a procedure manual for my current position. He said he did not have time to train each "new hire," nor could he rely on future employees to properly train their successors. "Without a procedure manual, it's like the old game of 'telephone,'" he explained. "Some of the message will be lost each time the job is turned over to the next person."

I understood and wrote the most accurate and detailed instructions I could, but I knew that even the procedure-manual approach was flawed. Those who read it would interpret the instructions according to their own experience. Also, the needs of the department would change over time. In spite of his hope to remain "hands off," the manager would have to stay involved.

The Bible, the procedure manual of life, is passed from one generation to the next, but in spite of the unique experiences of each reader and the changing needs of the world, every passage remains rich with truth and meaning. I believe that's because the Holy Spirit, the Manager, remains involved to provide insight and guidance to all who ask.

Prayer: Be near, Holy Spirit. Increase my understanding of the words of Scripture, the procedure manual of life; in Jesus' name. Amen

Epiphany[xxix]

... After Jesus' birth wise men from the east arrived in Jerusalem. They asked, "Where is the one who was born to be the king of the Jews? We saw his star rising and have come to worship him." ~ Matthew 2:1-2 (GW)

Christians celebrate the Festival of Epiphany to commemorate how Jesus was made known to the Magi. Every January 6th, we pause to remember, and to ponder that

- the Wise Men journeyed countless miles across the Holy Land,
- on hot, arid, desert routes,
- on dangerous highways beset with robbers,
- at great expense of time, resources, and energy,
- with ornery camels, and cumbersome supplies,
- living the caravan lifestyle,
- resting and replenishing supplies at dirty, smelly caravansaries,

all this to see Jesus with their very own eyes.

The expeditionary Wise Men, according to the Bible or widely-held tradition, were educated men, experts in the field of astronomy/astrology, scientists if you will. It appears they were both wealthy and powerful, possibly even royalty. And they knew the Messianic prophesies found in the Hebrew Scriptures.

One theory, although it cannot be proven, is that the Wise Men came from Ancient Babylon, a place world-renowned in its day for an advanced understanding of the solar system. It's possible the Wise Men were also descendants of the Hebrew captives taken to Babylon centuries earlier. That would explain how they knew Old Testament prophecy.

So, if they were smart and had so much power and wealth, why didn't they commission others – their students, or their servants, or a team of their royal subjects – to make the dirty, arduous journey and return with a full report?

They would not do that! No! They knew from observing the heavens, that something incredible had happened on earth – so incredible in the history of the universe, that even the stars in the heavens "celebrated" it. They wanted to see this marvelous, once-in-the-history-of-mankind event for themselves.

And was it because they wanted to prove some academic theory – the "connecting of dots" between science and religion? For personal fame? Fortune? No! They wanted to worship and honor the child, and personally present him their costly gifts.

Does this make any sense? Yes! It made perfect sense to them, because when they saw the child with their own eyes, they experienced an "epiphany," an understanding with clarity that Jesus is the Messiah!

Prayer: Creator of heaven and earth, thank you for working this same miraculous epiphany in our lives, today. For we, too, can understand with clarity: Jesus is the Messiah! Amen

Bread of Life[xxx]

Jesus told them, "I am the bread of life. Whoever comes to me will never become hungry, and whoever believes in me will never become thirsty."
~ John 6:35 (GW)

On our drive to Kansas this past spring, John and I stayed one night near Chillicothe, Missouri and discovered that Chillicothe is "The Home of Sliced Bread." This piece of history is recreated by local artist Kelly Poling in a mural that covers the entire side of a two-story building in downtown Chillicothe.

How many times – when someone is pleased to make some new discovery – do we hear the expression: "This is the greatest thing since the invention of sliced bread!" Now John and I stood in the very place where it all happened. On July 7, 1928 Otto Rohwedder's mechanized bread-slicing machine was used for the first time at the Chillicothe Baking Company.

Back in 1928, consumers were slow to accept the new product. They feared sliced bread might go stale quicker than a loaf kept whole. So the bakers installed a pin, which ran through the center of the loaf to hold the slices snugly together.

In today's verse, Jesus tells us that he is the Bread of Life. We are nourished as we remain in close contact with him through Bible study, prayer, and the fellowship of other believers – the "pins" that keep our faith fresh.

Furthermore, we can celebrate the Bread of Life by becoming a "living" mural in the public square – our faith and deeds portraying how Jesus is at work in our lives.

Prayer: Jesus, you are the bread of life. You preserve your Word for us and for future generations – as the Holy Spirit brings it to us, a slice at a time and fresh daily.

Orbits of Kingdom Work

Lordship of Jesus
(A 50-word or less devotion on a question Jesus asked)

Question: *"So why do you keep calling me 'Lord, Lord!' when you don't do what I say?"* ~ Luke 6:46 (NLT)

Devotion: Boss. Chief. Captain. Chancellor, Commander. Governor. President. Director. King. Queen. Master. Police Officer. Principal. Prime Minister. Czar. When they speak, we hop to! When they command, we obey. But sadly, we often name Jesus our "Lord" – with little intention to listen to or comply with his Word.

***

Limitations[xxxi]

He replied, "You give them something to eat." They answered, "We have only five loaves of bread and two fish..." ~ Luke 9:13 (NIV)

The disciples sized up the situation at hand. They had only five loaves and two fish and stood facing 5,000 people who were ready to faint with hunger. But they could not refuse to do what they had been asked. It was, after all, an assignment from Jesus – a Kingdom challenge, if you will. Their provisions seemingly not enough, they brought what they had to Him.

When we feel ill-equipped for our Kingdom challenges, we do well to follow the example of the first disciples, and in obedience, bring what we have to Jesus. He will bless what we offer and use it to accomplish his purposes. We mustn't project our limitations onto him "who is able to do immeasurably more than all we ask or imagine..." (Ephesians 3:20, NIV)

Prayer: Heavenly Father, we praise you for your greatness and thank you for your compassion. May we always remember that we are not alone and that you have the power to make our burdens light.

Workers Who Please God

Trustworthy messengers refresh like snow in summer. They revive the spirit of their employer. ~ Proverbs 25:13 (NLT)

New software would simplify the typing of repetitious legal documents. So my employer sent me, the law firm office manager, for training. When I returned to our office he wanted me to instruct the rest of his staff.

I enjoyed the challenge and found that six of the seven secretaries on the staff embraced the new system with optimism. They trusted my promise that the new software would eventually make their jobs easier.

I gave a lesson each morning, then circulated and provided individual coaching. For weeks, the office seemed to ring with the cry, "Helene, can you help me?"

One woman rejected my help, claiming she could learn better by trial and error. I saw her struggling and when her work began to pile up, I spoke with the boss. Since she'd been an excellent secretary, he gambled that she could learn the new system her way. He told me to continue offering help but not to press it.

I prayed she would become "teachable," but she remained stubborn. Her work fell further and further behind. Eventually, though she was capable of learning the new procedures, she resigned in defeat.

The experience taught me how frustrated God must feel when we turn a deaf ear to his offers of help. He knows the "system" and wants to teach us. He tells us to call out for his help – anytime, anywhere. He gives us the "software" – the tools to make our jobs easier – and he promises to reward us handsomely when our job is done. How foolish it is to "go it alone" and suffer defeat, when the Lord promises us victory.

Prayer: Lord, I long to be a worker with whom you are pleased. Help me, teach me, equip me to do your will.

Ecclesiastes 8:9-10 (NIV)

All this I saw, as I applied my mind to everything done under the sun. There is a time when a man lords it over others to his own hurt. Then too, I saw the wicked buried – those who used to come and go from the holy place and receive praise in the city where they did this. This too is meaningless.

Psalm 73:2-3, 16-17, 27-28 (NIV)

But as for me, my feet had almost slipped; I had nearly lost my foothold. For I envied the arrogant when I saw the prosperity of the wicked. When I tried to understand all this, it was oppressive to me till I entered the sanctuary of God; then I understood their final destiny. Those who are far from you will perish; you destroy all who are unfaithful to you. But as for me, it is good to be near God. I have made the Sovereign LORD my refuge; I will tell of all your deeds.

Time Management

Teach us to number our days, that we may gain a heart of wisdom.
~ Psalm 90:12 (NIV)

A friend who had moved to a seniors' community treated me to lunch in her new home. After we ate, she showed me the swimming pool, fitness center, library, game rooms, assisted living facilities, and nursing home. Her tour ended with a long walk outdoors and she pointed out various condos and private houses along the way.

"This is the home of a gentleman who once was president of XYZ Corporation," she announced. "And over here lives a man who owned a large engineering firm." Clara seemed to know everyone. Pointing to a townhouse adorned with colorful flower boxes and tinkling wind chimes, she said, "This place belongs to a lady who owned a ribbon and button business." My friend was obviously proud of her neighbors and the success they had achieved in their lives.

I didn't recognize any of the names she mentioned, but I began to think of the high-level executives I'd known in my career. Some had worked hard and deserved their success but others had climbed the corporate ladder by unscrupulous practices. I wondered where they were now.

Eventually we grow old, with our abilities and energies curtailed. Only *character* continues to gain strength and become more prominent – be it for good or for ill.

When I someday look back at my accomplishments, will it be with satisfaction or shame? Today's verse is a warning intended to spare us regret. Regardless of the days we have left, we should determine to use them well.

Prayer: Thank you, gracious Lord, for this admonition, that only what's done for Christ will last. Help us to use our energies wisely; in Jesus' name. Amen

Formula for Good Results

"Who despises the day of small things? Men will rejoice when they see the plumb line in the hand of Zerubbabel." ~ Zechariah 4:10 (NIV)

I signed up for adult education oil painting and imagined myself creating all kinds of masterpieces on canvas. But as the course progressed, I discovered it wasn't that easy. Week after week I agonized over the placement of every brush stroke and with increasing tenseness, achieved poorer and poorer results.

The instructor sensed my frustration and suggested I set simple goals and paint with abandon. Relieved of my self-inflicted pressure to produce a great work of art, and "throwing caution to the wind," I began to improve.

The words of our Lord to Zechariah hold a wonderful lesson for me. I tend to celebrate only when I have achieved my goal but today's scripture suggests we celebrate at the start. It tells us that the people rejoiced for the temple when Zerubbabel first handled the mason's tools. Day One of the project!

Parents rejoice when a child finds Middle C at that first piano lesson, or blows first-time bubbles at the town pool, or enters school on the first day of Kindergarten. Parents' early rejoicing sets the stage for the child's future. And all heaven rejoices the first time we repent and confess our need for Christ (Luke 15:10).

Certainly, I appreciate the praise of others when I produce good work. If that's my focus on day one, however, I've programmed myself for frustration and defeat. Praise God for his counsel to rejoice at each new beginning. If we begin with joy and enthusiasm, good results are much more attainable.

Prayer: Lord, help us to begin new projects and new assignments with joy and enthusiasm. Amen

Get Moving![xxxii]

Don't stay on your knees so long that you lose your ability to walk.

Then the LORD said to Moses, "Why are you crying out to me? Tell the people to get moving!" ~ Exodus 14:15 (NLT)

There's a time to pray and a time for action. Don't undertake one without the other.

***

Encouragement for Our Troops[xxxiii]

Dear Soldier,

Though you are far from home this Christmas, be assured American hearts hold you close. Your noble pursuits have taken you to dangerous places, and we pray you be kept safe – in mind, body, and spirit. Your cause is righteous; may the Lord bless your efforts with success.

Christmas reminds us that Christ came to bring peace to all peoples everywhere – the peace of God, known when hearts and lives are freed from the grip of evil.

May you, dear soldier, continue in good health, be spared injury, and return safely when your mission is accomplished. We pray that wisdom will guide our nation's leaders and that peace and security will be established around the globe in the new year. May the good Lord so fill your heart with His strength and grace that they overflow from your life into the lives of all you encounter.

Sincerely, Helene Kuoni, Allentown, PA

Marilyn's Shoe Bag

The stone the builders rejected has become the capstone; the LORD has done this, and it is marvelous in our eyes. ~ Psalm 118:22-23 (NIV)

My sister Marilyn had a shoe caddy hanging on the back of her clothes closet door for years. Made of quality material, it contained 16 sturdy pockets for eight pairs of shoes. With good intentions, she'd bought it to organize the footgear kicking around under her bed but it remained unfilled for many moons.

Then one day Marilyn decided to donate it to a church that needed "white elephants" for a fund-raiser. The morning of the event, Marilyn took the unused caddy to their fellowship hall, a place bustling with early shoppers scrambling to find treasures.

She was directed to a person off in one corner who flashed Marilyn a warm smile while completing a sale with someone else. Then, giving my sister her attention, she seemed to fall in love with Marilyn's donation.

"Oh, this is wonderful," she gushed, "and it has so many uses. This will be easy to sell." She mentioned some possibilities – "…shoes, of course, but it could also hang in a broom closet to store cleaning materials, and spray cans of furniture polish."

"It could hang in a garage," she noted, "for paint brushes and small tools. A gardener would love it! It could even hang in a crafts room to store scissors, measuring tapes, sewing machine bobbins, dressmaker's chalk."

What a salesperson she turned out to be. She continued listing all the possibilities until Marilyn started sharing her enthusiasm. "Wait a minute," my sister said, fondling the shoe caddy, "this is a very good thing. I could use it myself. I think I'll just keep it."

"Nothing doing," said the lady, grabbing it out of her hands. "This was donated to the church; I can't just give it away." They shared a good laugh. Then my sister paid $10 just to bring this marvelous thing home again.

Prayer: Lord, rescue me from idleness. Show me the possibilities for my life and put me to good use this day. Amen

***

Full Employment[xxxiv]

Then he said to his disciples, "The harvest is plentiful but the workers are few. Ask the Lord of the harvest, therefore, to send out workers into his harvest field." ~ Matthew 9:37-38 (NIV)

You know in your heart that the Lord has a job for you to do. His workers are never "excessed" out of his plans, or "downsized" out of his organization. Always remember, there's job security for all in the vineyards of the Lord.

Good Gossip

"...consider the voice of the singers at the watering places. They recite the righteous acts of the LORD, the righteous acts of his warriors in Israel. ..." ~ Judges 5:10-11 (NIV)

The sign above the muffin lady's counter read "Good Friends, Good Food, Good Gossip." While her husband prepared my egg sandwich back in the kitchen, I sipped my coffee, and she and I chatted a bit. I was vacationing in the Adirondack Mountains of upstate New York and enjoyed making a new friend. We commiserated about the rainy weather and discussed the local headlines and the dress sale at a nearby clothing store. When other customers came by, she introduced me to some of them and I enjoyed hearing the stories they had to share.

One of her regulars was a volunteer EMS worker who told us about an exciting rescue the night before. Another was a woman who, over many years, had delivered thousands of "Meals on Wheels" and could report on the progress being made by area shut-ins. Every customer who came along seemed to be actively engaged in helping other people and they all had great stories to tell. I was new to the community; I had nothing to add.

The musicians mentioned in today's verse congregated around the watering places and I imagine that their place of refreshment was also one of "Good Friends, Good Food, Good Gossip." They sang of God's power and might, and of his righteous acts among his warriors in Israel. They'd witnessed the Lord's work in the midst of the conflict and were excited to spread the news.

"Good gossip" results from having been somewhere or having done something exciting. Anyone actively engaged in the "good fight of faith" will have examples of God's power and love to share with others.

Prayer: Heavenly Father, help me to share the message of salvation with excitement and joy, for it is the best possible "good gossip" I can pass along.

Power Lunch[xxxv]

But I say, love your enemies! Pray for those who persecute you! In that way, you will be acting as true children of your Father in heaven...
~ Matthew 5:44-45 (NLT)

Management consolidated our Boston and New York offices, and I became Connie's supervisor. She was twenty years my senior, had previously been a journalist, and was uncooperative and incorrigible. My youth and insecurity were no match for this bold newspaperwoman. I finally spoke to the boss.

"Funny, you say things aren't working out," he said, "Connie's already complained."

"Complained? About me?" I felt outraged. My problematic subordinate had become my enemy!

"Invite her to lunch," he said. "Do something nice for her."

I hated the idea. For weeks I'd struggled with her obstreperous behavior. How could a sandwich help? But I had lunch with her anyway.

Over lunch I learned she'd moved to New York expecting to work for the department head, not a mid-level supervisor. I listened. I sympathized, realizing she'd relocated hundreds of miles under a false impression.

Lunch nourished a new relationship. Friendship soon blossomed, and I credit my boss's advice: "Do something nice for her," which echoed Jesus's admonition, "Do good to those who persecute you" (see Matthew 5:44).

~

Love those you find unlovable. The Lord has promised to reward you.

Fair Dealings[xxxvi]

Good comes to those who lend money generously and conduct their business fairly. ~ Psalm 112:5 (NLT)

"Want to buy cards?" he asked.

I couldn't believe it. A jacketless boy about seven years old stood outside my door late one snowy afternoon.

"You're selling greeting cards?" I asked incredulously. My thoughts raced. Did his parents approve his peddling? Alone? On a day like this? Were they destitute?

"Or, I can shovel," he offered.

"It'll snow all night. No point shoveling now."

"I'll come tomorrow!"

"Fine." What had I done? He was too young, too small.

He returned in the morning. But a high school boy saw him ring my bell and ran to the porch to vie for the job. I recognized the older boy as being from a nearby boarding school – one for delinquents referred by the courts.

"Work together?" I suggested. They agreed.

I watched from indoors and, when they finished, I gave them each $10. Then I asked the older one to stay. His expression clouded, as if he feared he'd done something wrong.

"Take this extra $10," I said. "The little boy was too young. You did the work and I want to be fair with you."

Appreciative, he smiled. "Thanks."

~

Be kind to the poor and treat others fairly, for both acts demonstrate love.

Goodness
(Essay)

The world celebrated the end of the war, yet winter winds whistled through the frozen, deserted streets of Siberia, and German prisoners of war cowered under the commands of their Russian taskmasters. Most worked in the salt mines, including the husband of my father's distant cousin.

For ten long years, no one – not his wife, not his parents, not his children, not anyone in his town – heard a word from or about him. And when he finally did return home, it was clear the experience had taken its toll.

He was thin and bent and had drawn into himself. A shell of a man, he was the language professor who had forgotten the art of social discourse and when he joined in conversation it certainly was not to divulge any of his POW experience.

He shouldn't have been a prisoner of war at all. Yes, he'd been a soldier in the German army but he was not a Nazi sympathizer. He'd been forced into service, the Third Reich believing this university professor would prove a great asset. But he didn't have a warrior's heart, nor could his spirit conform to the cause of his military leaders. Mild-mannered in all respects, he proved an easy capture.

Upon return, his neighbors were curious to learn details of his ten years but what did he have to tell? What could possibly distinguish one day in the salt mines from all the rest? It seemed he had nothing to say and those who were kindly disposed to his family did not press him. But when my dad visited his cousin in 1959, she divulged the one story she'd learned from her husband.

The "Herr Professor" had been several years into the hard labor of his captivity, when late one afternoon on a blustery and frigid day, he was commanded to scrub the marble steps of a municipal building. His garb shabby and tattered, the fingers on his gloves worn through, he knelt with a brush and scrubbed, and scrubbed, and scrubbed. Two guards stood nearly but remained more interested in their conversation and their cigarettes than in watching him perform his assignment.

Suddenly a woman appeared around the corner of the building. Dressed in a heavy woolen coat, she wore a black shawl overwrap, that covered her head as well as her shoulders and upper back. She was stooped – perhaps she was old, perhaps she was tired, perhaps she was trying to make herself small to go unnoticed by the authorities. She kept her face, her identity hidden. She emerged like a shadow out of the dark night, the air thick with dampness. The packed snow, on which she trod, muffled her steps.

She didn't say a word but let a crumpled newspaper drop as she passed the professor on his knees. For a second, he thought it an accident, but deep within, he knew her actions were intentional. He glanced over his shoulder. The soldier-guards were still engaged with each other. He sidled over to the crumpled mass. Hands trembling, he opened the paper. Inside he found a steaming baked potato.

Was the professor a man of faith? Had he prayed for help? For food? I do not know. What of the Russian peasant woman who showed him this kindness? I do not know. She might have been young. She might have been old. She might have been poor. She might have been sick. But this one thing I know: her heart was good. And she'd no hope of receiving thanks for her goodness. She shared anonymously with a stranger in need, even one her government deemed an enemy, and she put herself in great jeopardy for his sake.

The professor risked little that evening. Oh, the watchman could have taken the precious potato away, but the hungry prisoner would have been left no worse off than he'd been before.

The woman could have been caught and punished. The professor and she both knew that. He could not so much as give a nod in appreciation to his benefactress; she'd kept her eyes averted, her head turned away in her act of compassion and daring. No, the prisoner could not thank her. He could only repeat the story to his wife ten years later.

Her good deed received no thanks or recognition. But for sure it's been recorded in heaven. I believe the compassion she felt in her heart was of God. And I believe she'll wear a crown of glory into eternity for her goodness late one afternoon on a blustery and frigid day.

~

...but because you are willing, as God wants you to be; not greedy for money, but eager to serve;...when the Chief Shepherd appears, you will receive the crown of glory that will never fade away. ~ 1 Peter 5:2b, 4 (NIV)

[Delivered to Toastmasters Club]

Threatening Storm Clouds of Difficulty

The Puffback
(Personal Experience Story)

The flower shop clerk loved to chat. I thought she'd never finish writing up the order. Finally, she put her pen down and concluded the small talk by tilting her head, curling her lips tight in one corner, and rolling her eyes skyward. "Well, you know how husbands are!" she chuckled. *How husbands are? I'd just ordered flowers for my upcoming wedding. Hadn't she been paying attention?*

No one suspected how apprehensive I, as an older bride, felt about my new role. Could I do it all? Could I handle my responsibilities on the home front as well as the responsibilities of my career?

Daily I prayed for confidence as our big day approached and John continued to reassure me. Our wedding went smoothly and all my pre-marital jitters evaporated. I suddenly felt secure and on the path to a happy marriage.

We rented a quirky pre-Victorian house in the suburbs – a house with many rooms that had been added on to the original building over the years. The doorways between rooms had shallow steps to accommodate the different floor elevations. Often I'd stub my toe on the steps or bang my head on the low ceilings as I moved from one room to the next.

Our landlady, and former occupant of the house, was a veterinarian. The sign "Animal Clinic" still hung over the front porch and from time to time strangers appeared at our front door with their various pets.

One Saturday, while John was out shoveling snow, I came

downstairs carrying a basket of laundry in my arms and found a gentleman and his Great Dane sitting in our living room, "waiting their turn" to see the vet. And to add to the circus atmosphere of our lives, the animal clinic was on the market. Realtors stopped by on a moment's notice to give tours to prospective buyers. I must say John and I kept our senses of humor and we settled into a comfortable routine.

Then one cold night in January, I awoke at 3 A.M. with a throbbing headache. I pulled myself up from the pillow, but when I got out of bed, I collapsed to the floor. The thump of my fall woke John.

"What happened?" he said, jumping up. "What happened?"

I feel awful," I managed to say. "My head's splitting. The room's spinning. Make it stop," I begged.

"Do you think it's the flu?" he asked, still half asleep.

"No! It's not the flu! I never felt like this before!"

He squatted beside me in the dark and offered me his arm. I tried, but even with his help I couldn't rise. Suddenly the spinning accelerated. Sitting on the floor where I'd landed, I grabbed onto the dresser drawer handles in sheer terror.

"The room's whirling!" I shrieked. I dug my fingers into a dresser drawer, thinking that by clutching it tighter I could make the room slow down. "John, help me!" I cried. "The room is flying! I can't breathe. I'm so dizzy!"

Suddenly, John felt ill, too. Without another word, he took off for the basement, bounding as fast as he could down the two flights of stairs.

Hurry, John, hurry. Help me! O God, please save us. I don't want to die!... I, who had worried about "doing it all," could suddenly do nothing. I lost consciousness.

Downstairs John found the whole house filled with acrid smoke. He took the basement steps two at a time, flipped the oil burner switch to "off" and dashed back upstairs. Wasting no time, he banged his fists against the windows. We'd never been able to budge the sashes; they were painted shut over the years. John banged and banged.

"One more time!" he shouted, "then I'm throwing a chair through the glass." Sufficiently threatened, the window gave, and brisk air seeped through the shallow opening. John gave another yank and the window flung wide.

Cold! The night air was so beautifully cold and fresh. And it contained oxygen! As it filled my lungs, the ethereal "whirlpool" evaporated. I released my grip on the dresser drawer, and with John's assistance was able to stand. I vomited soot into the waste paper basket several times.

The insurance company called this experience a "puffback." Bricks, fallen down the 150-year old chimney, had caused the oil burner exhaust to fill the house and all but asphyxiate us in our sleep.

"Puffback" sounds too sweet a term to describe an episode that could have taken our lives. I shiver to think that John could have been overcome on his jaunt to the basement. If he had tripped and fallen on the stairs, our lifeless bodies would have been discovered the next day or whenever the realtor came by next.

In the morning, we were shocked to discover that a Halloween atmosphere of black cobwebs had taken over the basement and first floor. How great was our thanksgiving to God for sparing our lives, for drawing us ever closer to each other, and for giving me a sense that He would help us weather the storms of life together. I also prayed that someday we'd look back and be able to see humor in this experience.

Postscript

The house and everything in it had to be vacuumed and scrubbed, our clothes and linens all taken to the dry cleaners. A professional crew of four men, worked five days and it took a month before we saw our cat's true calico colors.

I saw a doctor who said my lungs would be fine and then prescribed something to prevent a sinus infection. So the Lord had preserved us through the night and spared us serious injury. It was good also to see how my new husband had handled the crisis. I could count on his help in my weak areas and insecurities.

Even my "bonus" prayer, that I'd someday see humor in the experience, was answered with remarkable speed – when I had a good laugh with the doctor.

~

(See *The Single Funniest Event in Our Marriage* on the next page.)

The Single Funniest Event in Our Marriage

(Email to Steve Doocy, co-host of *Fox & Friends* on cable TV and author of *Mr. & Mrs. Happy*. He'd requested stories from his television viewers.)

My husband John and I, a bit older than most couples when we married, began our life together in a 150-year old rented house. One cold January, in the wee hours of the morning, I woke with an excruciating headache, dragged myself to the bathroom, and collapsed on the return trip. John jumped out of bed when I crashed to the floor.

I kept pleading, "Make the room stop spinning!" but John couldn't figure out what was wrong with me – until he awoke more fully. Then he bounded down the two flights of stairs to the basement and found the house full of smoke (and carbon monoxide). He shut off the furnace, ran back upstairs and managed to pry open the painted-shut windows. Some bricks lining the 150-year old chimney had fallen and clogged the flue.

The next morning I visited "The Doctor is In." The doctor, a lovely middle-age woman, had been married many years. She listened to my lungs, checked my sinuses, and seemed interested, but a little perplexed as I related the details of the night before. I explained that John and I had just married and we didn't yet know each other's symptoms when we got sick. I told her how John thought I had the flu when he first came to my aid. "Oh, that explains it," she exclaimed with the joy of one who'd solved a great mystery. "That explains it," she said, "You're newlyweds. That's why he got out of bed to help you!"

~

Email response:

Helene – Thanks for the note. That's a great story! By the way I love the book you gave me [*Her Pen for His Glory*]. Thanks so much for your kindness. Steve

A Lesson from Arithmetic[xxxvii]

Do not be yoked together with unbelievers. For what do righteousness and wickedness have in common? Or what fellowship can light have with darkness? ~ 2 Corinthians 6:14 (NIV)

Before you marry, make sure both of you are whole because when you multiply fractions the result is always less.

Solution: Tell Jesus about your brokenness and he will make you whole.

***

God's Family

Lord, you have been our dwelling place throughout all generations. ~ Psalm 90:1 (NIV)

My husband and I recently acquired new computer software with which to build our genealogical family trees. A fun and rewarding project, we continue to discover fascinating history.

We both come from long lines of very fine people. What a heritage! What a blessing! What a thrill to discover the Christian faith goes back many generations in our families.

Exciting discovery as that is, it does not make us anything special. For God blesses everyone who comes to him through Christ and grafts us all into his family tree, dating back to the Old Testament heroes of the faith. He has a wonderful "family reunion" planned for us in heaven. What a magnificent past; what promise for a glorious future with his redeemed.

Flames of Prayer

"Take It to the Lord in Prayer"
From the hymn *What a Friend We Have in Jesus*
(A 50-word or less devotion on a question Jesus asked)

Question: *Turning around, Jesus saw them following and asked, "What do you want?"* ~ John 1:38 (NIV)

Devotion: Everyone wants something of eternal consequence: love, mercy, forgiveness, purpose for living, strength for a challenge. Do we articulate our needs to Jesus? Would we tell a store clerk, "I'm here to buy, but I don't know what?" Jesus calls us to new awareness. Pray, and strive to be specific.

***

Forward March!
(A 50-word or less devotion on a question Jesus asked)

Question: *Then the LORD said to Moses, "Why are you crying out to me? Tell the Israelites to move on."* ~ Exodus 14:15 (NIV)

Devotion: One of Martin Luther's famous mottos: "Ora et labore" (Latin), means "Pray and Work." Neither activity should stand alone. Furthermore, the Lord's words to Moses indicate that action can sometimes be urgent. We should not dawdle, even in prayer, when the Lord has made his directions clear to us.

Battle of the Buns[xxxviii]

"... So how much more will your Father in heaven give good things to those who ask him?" ~ Matthew 7:11 (GW)

One day during Lent, an exuberant lady in a bakery taught me to be more forthright when I pray. I had driven many miles out of my way to a bakery that bakes the most delicious hot cross buns. I'd planned to buy eighteen – six for my house and a dozen for my sister's. I arrived to find only fourteen on the shelf, so I requested them all. As the salesclerk started to box them, another shopper burst into the store.

"I hope you have hot cross buns for me," she called out, eyeing the near-empty tray. "I promised my husband – my husband of forty-six years! If I don't bring any home, my marriage is over!"

She began to plead. But when the clerk explained that the last buns had just been sold, she grew quiet. I couldn't bear it. I changed my order to twelve, leaving her the last two. She thanked me profusely, as we agreed these were, indeed, the best buns for miles around!

Later I pondered what the scene would have been like, had our roles been reversed. If she'd ordered the last buns, I likely would have remained my very reserved self and said nothing. Disappointed, I would have silently chastised myself for arriving second.

It certainly pays dividends to speak up, and that's especially true when we talk with the Lord. God doesn't want us to suffer silently, to chastise ourselves or to wallow in self-pity. He wants us to make our requests known. To paraphrase: If I, who am sinful, know how to give a couple of rolls to a stranger, how much more will my Father in heaven give to me when I ask Him?

Prayer: Heavenly Father, you graciously hear our prayers. Help us to speak up and ask for your help. We know it is in Jesus, the bread of heaven, that you satisfy our deepest longings.

Psalm 86:1-7 (GW)
A Prayer of David.

Turn your ear toward me, O LORD.
Answer me, because I am oppressed and needy.
Protect me, because I am faithful to you.
Save your servant who trusts you. You are my God.
Have pity on me, O Lord,
    because I call out to you all day long.
Give me joy, O Lord,
    because I lift my soul to you.
You, O Lord, are good and forgiving,
    full of mercy toward everyone who calls out to you.
Open your ears to my prayer, O LORD.
Pay attention when I plead for mercy.
    When I am in trouble, I call out to you
        because you answer me.

Good Counsel[xxxix]

Hear my prayer, O LORD; listen to my cry for mercy. In the day of my trouble I will call to you, for you will answer me. ~ Psalm 86:6-7 (NIV)

A friend recently attended a class on counseling in which the instructor cautioned the students never to give advice. "If you give advice," he warned, "you will be responsible whenever things turn out poorly. All you should do is listen and provide enough feedback to show you are paying attention and that you understand the problem."

I'm so glad this is not the way the Lord handles our concerns. When I bring a problem to God in prayer, it's because I need help! I want God to show me the way, to lead, direct, enlighten, and enable. How marvelous to know God doesn't just parrot an understanding of our concerns! Our Counselor hears when we call – and answers.

Prayer: Lord, thank you for your promise to hear every concern I bring in prayer and for the certainty of your help, comfort, and healing counsel; in Jesus' name. Amen

A Place of Prayer[xl]

On the Sabbath we went outside the city gate to the river, where we expected to find a place of prayer. ... ~ Acts 16:13 (NIV)

A few years ago, someone suggested that while we were on summer vacation, my husband John and I should take a canoe out on the lake at sunrise. Our friend and his wife had done this once, taking along their Bible and some devotional material. He described for us a tranquil scene with a fine mist rising from the water and the sun sparkling across the lake at dawn. Everything was so quiet, so peaceful, so still, and they read together, and prayed together, and felt near to God.

So the next Sunday we set our alarm clock and rose early. Boy, it was cold, but we were determined to have this wonderful experience. It was still dark and we could hardly see, but we managed to open the tool shed, find our personal floatation devices, and hike the canoe down to the shore. The lake was like glass. No one was around. We hopped into the canoe and paddled out. Boy, it was cold. It was peaceful all right, but it was also lonely. I started to think distracting thoughts.

I'm sorry to report I did not find the experience very satisfying, but I did learn two important lessons. First, the "place of prayer" can be different for different people, and second, every one of us needs a place free of distractions if we are to draw near to the Lord.

Prayer: Heavenly Father, help each of us to find that special "place of prayer." Draw near to us as we meet you there this Lenten Season; in Jesus' name. Amen

Lugar para la oración[xli]

Hechos 16:13
Y el sábado salimos fuera de la puerta, junto al rio, donde suponiamos que había un lugar de oración.

Hace algunos años en el verano, alguien sugerió que mi esposo y yo dieramos un paseo al lado del río durante la salida del sol. Nuestro amigo y su esposa lo habían hecho alguna vez, con su Biblia y devociones, y dijo que fue una experienca tremenda. Describió la vista tranquila con una niebla encima del agua y un sol brillante durante la madrugada. Todo era tan tranquilo, tan quieto, tan silencioso, y leyeron juntos, oraron juntos, y se sintieron muy cerca de Dios.

Entonces el próximo domingo nos despertamos muy temprano. Hacía mucho frío, pero quisieramos tener esta experiencea tan maravillosa. Era oscuro todavía y casi no podiamos ver, pero encontramos el camino al río. El agua era muy tranquila. Nadie estaba allí. Nos sentamos encima de una roca grande. Hacía mucho frio.

Era tranquilo, pero también era aislado. Empecé a pensar: Hoy osos negros cerca de nosotros? Ellos pueden nadar, si? Hacía mucho frío esa mañana.

No me gustó mucho esta experiencia, pero aprendí dos cosas muy importantes. Primero, el "lugar para la oración" puede ser distinto para cada persona, y segundo, que cada persona necesita un lugar que no tiene distracciones para acercarse a Dios.

Oración: Nuestro Señor, ayudanos, encontrar este "lugar pera la oración" tan especial. Encuentranos allá durante este tiempo de oración antes de la navidad. En el nombre de Jesucristo. Amen

When Timing was Everything[xlii]

What the wicked dreads will overtake him; what the righteous desire will be granted. ~ Proverbs 10:24 (NIV)

My long-time employer announced plans to relocate out of state but promised everyone their positions, salaries, and benefits until the move three years later. Normally, this would have caused me great consternation, but I had too much on my mind. My sister Dorothy had just died. I had to grieve and take care of her affairs. I didn't think about my future. I prayed, "Help me, Lord, to find a good lawyer. Help me to respond to all the letters of condolence... "

About a month later, I awoke one morning with ideas exploding in my mind like an army of fireflies on a hot summer evening. *Company's leaving...fulfill old dream... study communication... all benefits still available... tuition refund plan... find school... do it now!*

I knew the Lord was directing my thoughts, so I hopped out of bed and headed for the library. From all appearances, the timing was wrong. Graduate-level study is rigorous. Wasn't I physically exhausted, emotionally spent, and burdened will all sorts of extra responsibilities?

At the library I discovered a course of study that appealed to me at Fairfield University, only an hour's drive from home. Within a week I had arranged all the necessary paperwork.

Less than four months after my sister's unexpected death, I sat in a classroom, with a blank notebook opened in front of me and a pencil poised in my hand. The professor lectured for two hours but I didn't hear a word, nor did I record anything in my notebook.

Two days later I again sat with my pen poised and returned home with an empty notebook. The third class, however, I began to concentrate, take notes, and enjoy the course. Going to class redirected my focus and actually helped me deal with my grief. I thanked the Lord, that everything had fallen into place so quickly.

Halfway through the semester, our professor began class with a serious announcement. The college planned to close its Graduate School of Communication and, effective that day, would consider no new applicants. Only those already enrolled could complete the degree. My heart raced with excitement to realize that God had led me to this program just in time to fulfill my childhood desire to study communication and become a writer.

Lesson

The "desires of our hearts" are also prayers, oftentimes more weighty than words strung together in beautiful prose. When emotional stress and the burdens of life pressed in and kept me from articulating my specific need for career direction, God still knew the desires of my heart and led me in the way I should go just as Solomon wrote [in Proverbs] so long ago. When my own reasoning ability would have said, "wait," the Lord got me going, and just at the right time.

He will guide you also as you surrender the desires of your heart to Him. He delights in granting His righteous children what He knows is best for them.

Prayer is the soul's sincere desire, uttered or unexpressed; the motion of a hidden fire that trembles in the breast.   – James Montgomery

God's Promises and Power in Creation

The Sky-High Promise[xliii]

And God said, "This is the sign of the covenant I am making ... for all generations to come: I have set my rainbow in the clouds ... Never again will the waters become a flood to destroy all life." ~ Genesis 9:12-13a, 15b (NIV)

It was okay to tell a lie when I was a kid – as long as your fingers were crossed behind your back. Every child in the neighborhood knew that. It was the "safe" way to fib, to fool your friends, or to make promises you had no intention of keeping. If those fingers were crossed behind your back, you could lie without fear of guilt or reprisal.

The idea came from the streets, as each generation of children passed the belief on to the next, but I soon discovered it was contrary to what my teachers taught in Sunday school. Lying was always wrong, for it is not God's way.

God never lies. He does not fib to us, trick us, or make promises that he doesn't keep. When he spoke to Noah after the Deluge, he promised never to flood the world again, and to seal the covenant, he placed a rainbow in the sky.

The rainbow was his signature on the bottom line of a contract with mankind, and the ink is still fresh and visible to us today. It's there whenever we come through stormy weather and need reassurance. When life gets rough, when the clouds gather and the rains pour down, I hold onto the certainty of that promise. For the rainbow given to Noah, is a sign of God's steadfastness to this day.

God is mighty; his love is immeasurable and unending; and his promises are sure. He promised to send Jesus, to send the Holy Spirit, to be with us always, and to prepare a place for us in heaven. I can't subscribe to the "wisdom" of the streets when God's promise is in the sky.

Deuteronomy 29:29 (GW)

Some things are hidden. They belong to the LORD our God. But the things that have been revealed in these teachings belong to us and to our children forever. We must obey every word of these teachings.

Hebrews 4:12-13 (NIV)

For the word of God is living and active. Sharper than any double-edged sword, it penetrates even to dividing soul and spirit, joints and marrow; it judges the thoughts and attitudes of the heart. Nothing in all creation is hidden from God's sight. Everything is uncovered and laid bare before the eyes of him to whom we must give account.

God's Secret Work[xliv]

As you do not know...how the body is formed in a mother's womb, so you cannot understand the work of God,... ~ Ecclesiastes 11:5 (NIV)

My friend meant well when she asked, "Is your arm healing?" My broken arm had been in a cast for three weeks and was as immobile as the day the orthopedist had wrapped it up. I couldn't give her a progress report. Though I'd learned new ways to bathe, dress, and open a jar, I had no way of knowing what my bones were doing. I had asked the Lord for healing, but beyond that, all I could do was wait and trust.

God works in secret on broken bones, in secret inside a mother's womb, and in secret inside the seeds in the farmer's field. God also works in the secret places of our souls, bringing us to repentance. God works in the secret places of our minds and hearts, giving us ideas, hopes, and dreams.

I couldn't answer my friend, but I thanked her for asking. Her question led me to a greater appreciation of our Creator God.

Prayer: Heavenly Father, thank you for working in our lives even when we are not aware of all that you do to sustain us, body and soul; in Jesus' name. Amen

I'm Listening[xlv]

The heavens declare the glory of God; the skies proclaim the work of his hands ... Their voice goes out into all the earth, their words to the ends of the world. ~ Psalm 19:1, 4 (NIV)

I shoveled for an hour, but the heavy snow still covered most of the driveway. I stopped to rest and said to myself, "If only the sun would come out." As if on cue, the sky brightened, the clouds parted, and shadows appeared on the snow. I laughed at the timing.

The storm had hit the Midwest as well and I wondered if my friends in Ohio were also shoveling at that moment. I thought of others I knew in other states and imagined them all shoveling right along with me and how the sunshine could help us all regardless of the miles separating our various driveways. How marvelous is the sun! How exciting to stop and consider it!

The skies "spoke" to me that day as they speak simultaneously to everyone on earth. To some they speak through sunshine, to some through the clouds and rain, to some through the moon and stars, but everywhere they reveal the marvels of God's creation. Too often I take it for granted but today I stopped to listen and heard the skies' glorious proclamation.

Prayer: Heavenly Father, help me to pause more often, to see more fully, and to appreciate more deeply, the wonders of Your creation; in Jesus' name. Amen

The Lover's Promise

I will also give him the morning star. ~ Revelation 2:28 (NIV)

"I, Jesus, have sent my angel to give you this testimony for the churches. I am the Root and the Offspring of David, and the bright Morning Star." ~ Revelation 22:16 (NIV)

I sat on the sofa with tissues in my lap, staring at the television as the movie credits scrolled by. The old love story had moved me to tears. Dabbing my eyes, I thought of the young hero's ardent proposal. "Marry me," he said, "and I'll give you the sun, moon and stars."

The story had been filmed in the 1940s and I wondered if his proposal was typical of that time. Is anyone today so poetic? I'm certain such promises come from the strongest of emotions. Young lovers desire only the best for their sweethearts, the best the world has to offer.

God's love is like that but even more so. In today's scripture passage, the Lord asks us to remain faithful and promises to give us the morning star. It's a promise that comes from a love that's extreme and we can count on its being fulfilled. The morning star that God promises is not simply one of the millions he's created to light the nighttime sky, though he could do that. It is *the* Morning Star – Christ himself.

Prayer: Heavenly Father, creator of the galaxies, help us to remain faithful. Out of your deep love, you have given your children the Morning Star, Jesus Christ; in his name. Amen

Mark 4:35-41 (NIV)

That day when evening came, he said to his disciples, "Let us go over to the other side." Leaving the crowd behind, they took him along, just as he was, in the boat. There were also other boats with him. A furious squall came up, and the waves broke over the boat, so that it was nearly swamped. Jesus was in the stern, sleeping on a cushion. The disciples woke him and said to him, "Teacher, don't you care if we drown?"

He got up, rebuked the wind and said to the waves, "Quiet! Be still!" Then the wind died down and it was completely calm.

He said to his disciples, "Why are you so afraid? Do you still have no faith?"

They were terrified and asked each other, "Who is this? Even the wind and the waves obey him!"

Mightier than Creation

Mightier than the thunder of the great waters, mightier than the breakers of the sea – the Lord on high is mighty. Your statutes stand firm; holiness adorns your house for endless days, O LORD. ~ Psalm 93:4-5 (NIV)

I remember a New Year's Eve when weather forecasters predicted a serious winter storm. I hurried to the supermarket for bread, eggs, and milk and after scurrying for a parking space, joined the throng vying for shopping carts.

The automatic door swung open and I was greeted by two handwritten posters, written no doubt by some harried employee worn down by customers' questions. The first read "Emergency Storm Supplies (batteries, candles, matches, etc.) Aisle 7." The second sign, propped directly beneath the first, read "Party Supplies (balloons, hats, noise-makers, confetti) Aisle 10."

Some customers shopped to prepare for the storm, and others to prepare for a party. Some people, no doubt, visited both aisles.

We scurry about when fearful, as well as when we party. It is good to remember God's steadfastness at both times. Our Lord is all powerful and holy. His laws and his love can be relied upon. He will not be tossed about by anything in his creation.

Prayer: Mighty Lord, creator of the world, stay near us always. Then when we face the storms of life, we will know your holy presence; in Jesus' name. Amen

"Let All Mortal Flesh Keep Silence"
An ancient chant based on Habakkuk 2:20

But the LORD is in his holy temple; let all the earth be silent before him.
~ Habakkuk 2:20 (NIV)

On vacation many years ago, my dad drove the family up New Hampshire's Mount Washington, an experience I will never forget. We arrived late afternoon as bad weather settled in around the summit. The park rangers allowed us to enter but then closed the gate to any additional tourists that day.

We soon learned that once a car embarks on the narrow, uphill road, there is no turning back. It doesn't matter if you feel your heart in your throat, or your knuckles freeze in fear around the steering wheel. The only way down the mountain is to first reach its peak. What a relief to arrive safely. Then we cautiously began our descent.

We stopped at a scenic overlook above the tree line because the guidebook promised a magnificent view. When we stepped out of the car and peered over the mountain ledge, we saw nothing, so dense was the evening fog. We gazed into an abyss and an eerie stillness engulfed my family. No one said a word and that's when I heard something I'd never heard before: SILENCE! I didn't like it. It overpowered me, made me feel so alone. I had to speak, to make some noise to break the awful silence.

Now that I've experienced Mount Washington in the fog, I better understand the prophet Habakkuk's awe-filled cry. He warns: "The Lord is in his holy temple, let all earth be silent before him!" Oh, the reverence, the fear and trembling! Can a person survive? Only God himself could provide for us.

God saved us and called us to be holy, not because of what we had done, but because of his own plan and kindness. Before the world began, God planned that Christ Jesus would show us God's kindness. Now with the coming of our Savior Christ Jesus, he has revealed it. Christ has destroyed death, and through the Good News he has brought eternal life into full view. (2 Timothy 1:9-10, GW)

Praise be to the Lord for his marvelous mercy and provision! For Christ is my Savior and I'm no longer alone in the silence. He lifts the fog and brings eternity into view.

Prayer: Lord, you alone are awesome. All creation points to your great power and glory.

Uphill Battles and Bountiful Blessings[xlvi]

> I spoke to you when you were born. Be still.
> Know I am God. I speak to you through
> the trees of the forests. Be still. Know I am
> God. I speak to you through the valleys
> and the hills. Be still. Know I am God.
> I speak to you through the waves of the
> sea. Be still. Know I am God. I speak
> to you through the dew of the morning.
> Be still. Know I am God. I speak
> to you through the peace of the evening.
> Be still. Know I am God.
> I speak to you through the brilliant stars.
> Be still. Know I am God. I will speak to
> you when you are alone. Be still. Know
> I am God. I will speak to you through-
> out Eternity. Be still. Know I am God.
> ~ The Essene Gospel of Peace.

Pace. It seemed that's all I did the hot, humid month of June when I was twenty years old and halfway through my college education. Every day, I watched for the letter carrier to come down the block, and the interminable wait dragged on. I tried to keep myself busy – reading, embroidering, sweeping the sidewalk, helping my mom with chores around the house – whatever I could find to do close to home. My summer job kept me busy on weekends, but weekdays afforded me plenty of time to stew. So that's what I did. Where was it? Where was my acceptance letter?

In May, I'd graduated from junior college and all the hustle and bustle of campus life and my various classes came to a sudden halt. For two years, I'd worked hard to meet the course requirements of my

God's Promises and Power in Creation

Associate's degree, and simultaneously to fulfill the requirements for entrance to a college of the City University of New York. I'd applied myself to my studies and made good grades. I'd prepared well and felt my acceptance to Hunter College a sure thing. So where now was that delinquent acceptance letter?

After weeks of greeting our mail carrier with "Anything from Hunter?" and his shaking his head in reply, he finally "delivered" the end of June. He approached our house with a grin, the coveted letter in hand, and chuckled when I grabbed the envelope and ripped it open right there on the sidewalk.

This was to be a moment of triumph, of success achieved. My hands shook with excitement as I tore back the flap, but when I read the curt message inside, I was stunned. "We regret to inform you…" My mind raced as only a twenty-year-old's can. *What? This cannot be happening. This violates all cosmic rules! What happened to the law of cause and effect?* I had met the requirements and given it my best effort. I should have attained the predicted outcome. Little did I know or appreciate how blessed I'd been that it had always happened that way before. How simple! How logical! How in control I'd always felt! Life had been difficult at times and frequently required great effort, but it had always played fair and followed my same straightforward formula for success.

I had no idea what to do next. Acceptance to Hunter College, back in the 1960s, was like winning a scholarship. No tuition! And that certainly would help make up for the expenses of my freshman and sophomore years. My parents planned to put all four of their daughters through higher education. I couldn't ask them to spend more money for mine now that the free tuition of Hunter was being denied.

With the fall semester only two months away, I had no time to apply elsewhere. If college was no longer possible, could I find a job? I had majored in liberal arts and except for my limited typing ability, I had no marketable skills. Besides, I was timid and the "real world" frightened me. I had made no contingency plans. Because I had done well, taken the required courses, achieved the required grades, and was a resident of New York City, didn't Hunter have to accept me? After all, I had played by their rules for two years.

I ran into the house, letting the screen door bang behind me, and telephoned the Hunter Admissions Office. "You lack the foreign language credits," they informed me. "But that's impossible," I protested. "I completed two semesters of German and plan to take the third term in my junior year." They would not budge but maintained that some technicality kept them from accepting my first semester of German.

Next, I telephoned my junior college and questioned the academic dean. He graciously contacted Hunter on my behalf, only to learn that Dean Hollinghurst, the one person who could have provided some guidance, had gone on vacation. Completely frustrated with all the people who might have helped, I turned my thinking toward God. I believed when a person tried their hardest, God blessed their efforts with success. My goal was honorable and I had the ability to attain it. Was I asking too much? For days I struggled with God and poured over other college catalogs at the library, searching in vain for a workable solution. For days, I examined my motives, my methods, and myself. *What was the magic formula for miracles?* I wondered.

No answers, no insight came all week. Frustrated and exhausted, I went to my room after lunch one day, closed the door, and fell to my knees. This was not my customary posture for praying but I wanted to submit to God's will and this seemed appropriate. With tears in my eyes, and my knees pressing against the hard wooden floor, I prayed, "Dear Lord, I don't know what to do. I don't know if I'm supposed to continue my studies or find a job. I don't know where I can go to school. I don't know where I can go to work. I'm in such a muddle. But the Bible says you have a plan for my life. Help me to be still so I can discover what you want me to do. Lord, I put it all into your hands." At wits' end, my emotions taut, my soul aching with despair, I gave it all up to God.

Later that afternoon, my older sister came home from her teaching job. "How 'bout a swim at Blue Mountain Lake?" she suggested. It was the last day of the school year, and she was ready for the summer fun to begin. I grabbed my suit and off we went. The lake, only forty-five minutes from home, might well have been halfway around the globe, so far did I feel transported from my troubles. The sunshine sparkled across the water. The blue sky played backdrop to an occasional cumulus cloud. I laid on my back on the soft and glistening sand. Motionless, I let the quiet summer breezes blow over me. Time seemed suspended as I stared into the clear sky and thought of nothing at all.

I had relinquished my problem and my future to God, and without any effort of will on my part, the anxiety drifted away with nature's breeze. So complete was my mental and emotional transformation, I forgot I ever had a problem to solve. When we returned home, I felt refreshed and rejuvenated.

Mom was waiting at the front door with some stunning news to share. "Helene," she beamed, "you'll never believe it. Dean Gabbert called. He reached Dr. Hollinghurst this afternoon and she'll admit you in September. All you have to do is find an approved German class this summer and complete it successfully."

I could not believe my ears. Two years of planning and studying, a month of waiting, and a week of fretting, had changed nothing. Then, I relinquished my efforts to the Lord, and all was turned around in an afternoon – an afternoon I had spent lost in the tranquility of God and his creation.

My story doesn't end there. I had to find an approved course, and, having found one, plead for admission to a class that was already overenrolled. I had to find transportation to the school because I didn't have a car or a driver's license. And finally, I had to work hard to pass a difficult course. Nineteenth-century German literature was no piece of apple strudel (especially without a nineteenth-century German dictionary). My expertise was not, and never will be, nineteenth-century anything, no less a foreign language. I had to look up every word I read, and after each two-hour class and the two-hour roundtrip commute, my homework took me three hours each day and six on weekends.

What a summer I spent! Nevertheless, I knew God had me back on the right path. I completed the six-week course with a B and, in September, began my junior year at Hunter College.

It had been a summer of uphill battles, but it taught me a great lesson. Life is not under my control. I can apply myself, work hard, set and achieve one goal after the next, but it is God who establishes my steps and bestows his blessings. The same God who created the universe and set the moon and stars in their courses, created me. His greatest desire is for me to turn to him in every circumstance of my life. When I dwell in Him, I receive His blessings.

Sunset Rest

Matthew 11:28-30 (NIV)

"Come to me, all you who are weary and burdened, and I will give you rest. Take my yoke upon you and learn from me, for I am gentle and humble in heart, and you will find rest for your souls. For my yoke is easy and my burden is light."

Relax[xlvii]

He makes me lie down in green pastures, he leads me beside quiet waters, he restores my soul… ~ Psalm 23:2-3 (NIV)

I recently cleaned out my jewelry box and came upon an old gold chain that had been in my family for many years. I never wore the necklace but kept it because of its age. I hope someday to find a relative who would enjoy having this heirloom.

In the meantime there was a problem: it was tangled in a million knots and the more I tried to untangle it, the more snarled it became. I twisted it one way, then another. I analyzed several of the loops and tried again, but instead of unwinding the mess, I made it worse. I took it to the window for more light and stuck a straight pin into one of the tiny, slippery links, hoping to keep some part of the chain stationary, but the harder I tried, the worse the tangle became.

I felt completely stressed and then the phone rang. My friend listened to my frustration and told me she'd once taken a knotted chain to a jewelry store. The jeweler took the chain into his hands and within minutes, right before her eyes, he removed all the knots until the chain lay flat on the counter – smooth, rehabilitated, restored to new life.

"How did he do it?" I asked in amazement.

"He relaxed the chain," she said, "Instead of pulling on the knots, he placed it on a flat surface and rolled the knots gently to loosen them up."

I never forgot that lesson – and I've straightened out many a tangled chain since that time by simply "relaxing" the chain.

This is how the Lord often works when I come to him feeling all taut and tangled up. When I put myself into his hands, he takes me to a quiet place and there "beside the still waters, he restores my soul." I find rest with him. God makes the rough places smooth. No longer tied in knots, I'm restored to new life and purpose.

Prayer: Heavenly Father, when I put myself in your hands, I avoid the stressful "knots" of worry, fear, and wrong thinking. Give me the faith and courage I need to more fully rely on your leading day by day; in Jesus' name. Amen

Neglected Miracle[xlviii]

The LORD replied, "My Presence will go with you, and I will give you rest." ~ Exodus 33:14 (NIV)

Then, because so many people were coming and going that they did not even have a chance to eat, he said to them, "Come with me by yourselves to a quiet place and get some rest." ~ Mark 6:31 (NIV)

I made a long list one morning of the things I wanted to accomplish during the day. The list included exercise, so I decided to walk to town to mail some letters. It was afternoon before I headed out and I was feeling very tired from all the housework I'd done that morning. But I felt compelled to accomplish everything on my list and could only do so by keeping at it non-stop.

For the most part, my route to the post office was downhill. Halfway there, I met a young woman coming from the opposite direction with her son, his little legs pumping uphill on a tricycle. About four years old, he looked especially cute with his curly locks hanging just below the rim of a shiny new helmet. As we were about to pass each other, he hopped off the bike, gazed up at his mother and pleaded, "Mom, I need a nap."

What a smart little fellow! He certainly showed greater wisdom than I, for I hadn't allowed myself a break all day. I'd forgotten that God not only allows us a rest, he prescribes it. For didn't Jesus, recognizing his disciples' fatigue, say, "Come with me by yourselves to a quiet place and get some rest"?

A rest does us so much good. No matter how spent we are from the rigors of the day, when we lay our bodies down and get a good night's sleep, we arise in the morning and find our energies replenished. I don't understand how that happens. I just know, it is one of the many miracles God works in our lives every day, and that day I'd foolishly neglected his precious gift, his miracle called "rest."

The Unopened Gift

"Six days you shall labor, but on the seventh day you shall rest; even during the plowing season and harvest you must rest." ~ Exodus 34:21 (NIV)

In vain you rise early and stay up late, toiling for food to eat – for he grants sleep to those he loves. ~ Psalm 127:2 (NIV)

Thomas Edison invented the first incandescent lamp on October 21, 1879 and changed civilization forever. Electricity permeates every field of endeavor around the world – science, medicine, education, health, business, industry, finance, recreation, food, farming; you name it!

With the flip of a switch, we extend our workday and accomplish so much good. But despite all the good, electric light bulbs can be a bane to many. We over-commit. Our employers, our friends, our families, even our churches can make us feel guilty if we do not use our "spare" time for their benefit.

It is good to reflect on what God requires of us and to remember that rest is God's gift to those he loves.

Prayer: Loving Master, thank you for the work you assign us daily and for your gift of rest at the end of each day; in Jesus' name. Amen

Memories

He remembers his covenant forever, the word he commanded, for a thousand generations. ~ Psalm 105:8 (NIV)

My Aunt Lilly at 95, mailed a birthday card to someone who was a friend since high school. The woman now lived several states away and telephoned Lilly when she received the card. She didn't call just to say thank you, however. "The reason I'm calling," she said, "is to ask you a question. Did I turn 94 or 95? I can't remember."

We all have things we don't remember but it is comical when we forget something as personal as our own age. It's comical, but not really that important.

What's important to remember is the love of God, and the salvation we have because Christ atoned for our sins. That's our most personal – and most precious – possession. Even if someday our memories should fail us, we can rest assured that the Lord will never forget us, his redeemed.

Prayer: Loving Father, as we grow older and more forgetful, help us always to remember that Jesus died in our place. You will never forget us, your children; in Jesus' name. Amen

Mary at Prayer[xlix]

The purpose of prayer is that we get ahold of God, not of the answer.
– Oswald Chambers

"Can you come over?" she asked on the phone.

I couldn't refuse Mary. Our families were lifelong friends, and she was ill. I went immediately.

We chatted endlessly and reminisced about parents and siblings and the wonderful times our families had shared. We talked about my sister, Dorothy, and her sister, Pat – both had died in their forties. We talked about Christ and Heaven and being reunited someday with those we loved so much.

"Can we pray?" she asked hesitantly. "Like conversation with God? Aloud?" I took her hands into mine and silently planned how to begin, how to phrase each request, but she surprised me by starting first. "Heavenly Father," she prayed, "thank you for my friend and for her beauty."

It startled me. What was she saying? I thought we were to petition the Lord on her behalf. She continued her thanksgiving – for husband, children, doctors, parents, sisters, brothers. So caught up in counting her blessings, she asked for nothing – not health, not even relief from the pain.

We prayed every time I visited after that, and Mary always "entered His gates with thanksgiving." Her skin was pale and her strength ebbing, but as she approached the Lord, a brightness and beauty appeared on her face.

I treasure the memory of Mary at prayer. I know when the Lord took her home, her face must have shone with beauty, and as she had done so many times before, she "entered His courts with praise."

When Moses came down from Mount Sinai with the two tablets of the covenant law in his hands, he was not aware that his face was radiant because he had spoken with the Lord. ~ Exodus 34:29 (NIV)

Thought ... Are you transformed when you pray? When you look to God, for *Who* He is and not for *what* He gives, you become radiant (Psalm 34:5, NIV).

Collection of Treasures

And he will send his angels and gather his elect from the four winds, from the ends of the earth to the ends of the heavens. ~ Mark 13:27 (NIV)

I sat on the edge of the bed one morning, and it broke – not because of my weight but because of a "manufacturer's defect." We reported the problem and to our surprise, the store manager told us we could choose anything of equal value in his showroom to make up for the loss. We couldn't believe his generosity! My husband said he could patch up the broken bed, so not needing a new one, we chose instead a large curio cabinet for the living room.

I had long wanted a central place to display all my valuable "stuff." Until now it was spread throughout the house. No longer would my knickknacks and family heirlooms stand in places where they could be knocked over and broken.

I had great fun gathering my collection of treasures, polishing up all the various pieces, and putting everything together in the new display case. I enjoyed arranging the figurines I'd acquired over many years, from different places around the world and from different times in family history. When the job was completed, it seemed a heavenly display!

Someday the Lord will bring his own together from various times in history and from diverse places around the globe. He will remove us from the dangerous location of this world. He will "polish" us up and assign us a place in his mansions of gold (John 14:2, KJV). In exchange for Christ's brokenness on the cross, we are given a home in his heavenly collection.

Prayer: Generous Father, my new curio cabinet was not free. Neither is heaven. Jesus paid for it with his life, broken on the cross. As he gives the gift of salvation freely to me, help me to be generous in sharing the Good News with others.

Harvest of Salvation

Psalm 32 (NIV)
Of David. A *maskil*.

Blessed is he whose transgressions are forgiven,
   whose sins are covered.
Blessed is the man
   whose sin the LORD does not count against him
   and in whose spirit is no deceit.
When I kept silent, my bones wasted away
   through my groaning all day long.
For day and night your hand was heavy on me;
   my strength was sapped
   as in the heat of summer.
Then I acknowledged my sin to you
   and did not cover up my iniquity.
I said, "I will confess my transgressions to the LORD" -
and you forgave the guilt of my sin.
Therefore let everyone who is godly pray to you
   while you may be found;
   surely when the mighty waters rise,
   they will not reach them.
You are my hiding place;
   you will protect me from trouble
   and surround me with songs of deliverance.
I will instruct you and teach you in the way you should go;
   I will counsel you and watch over you.
Do not be like the horse or the mule,

which have no understanding
but must be controlled by bit and bridle
or they will not come to you.
Many are the woes of the wicked,
  but the LORD's unfailing love
surrounds the man who trusts in him.
Rejoice in the LORD and be glad, you righteous;
  sing, all you who are upright in heart!

In Need of a Good Scrubbing[1]

But who can endure the day of his coming? Who can stand when he appears? For he will be like a refiner's fire or a launderer's soap.
~ Malachi 3:2 (NIV)

When life's pressures mount, when we're weary from the race, when friends fail us, when we face seemingly insurmountable obstacles – at such times we might say, "I feel like a dishrag." A dishrag is a flimsy thing. Even when it's new, a dishrag is limp. Soon it's also thin, torn, dirty, floppy, and soppy from use. Yes, a dishrag is a fitting metaphor for how we feel when faced with the rigors of life.

Malachi tells us that when God comes calling, only that which is holy can be in his presence. Even if our threadbare selves were scrubbed with harsh soap, twisted and wrung, beaten against the rocks to make us clean – even then we would not be worthy or able to stand in the glory of the Lord's presence.

Furthermore, we cannot make ourselves acceptable by pointing out all the pots we've scrubbed, or all the good uses we've been put to. For "all our righteous acts are like filthy rags" (Isaiah 64:6a, NIV). Our only hope is to come to Christ, confess our condition, and receive the garments of salvation. Only then will we "hang out" in God's sunlight and enjoy the refreshing Spirit breezes.

Prayer: O Holy God, I confess my sin to you. Cleanse me and clothe me in the garments of salvation available only through your Son, Jesus Christ. Amen

~

In need of a Good Scrubbing (Chinese)

詩篇　32：1－7

今日の思索：　彼の来る日に誰が身を支えうるか。彼の現れるとき、誰が耐えうるか。彼は精錬する者の火、洗う者の灰汁のようだ。マラキ　3：2

　生活の圧力に押し潰されそうになる時、競争に疲れ果てた時、友に見捨てられた時、耐え難い障害に直面した時、そんな時に我等は良く言います：「皿洗いの布のようだ、」「皿洗いの布」は薄っぺらな物です。それは新しい物でも草臥れた感じがします。それは真に、薄くなったり、破れたり、汚れたり、使って居る内にグシャグシャになります。そうです、「皿洗いの布」は我等が生活の厳しさに直面した時の譬えにぴったりです。

　神が招きに来られた時、聖なる者だけが神の前に出る事が出来るとマラキは我等に言っています。仮令、我等が擦り切れる程荒い石鹸をつけて洗われても、ねじられて、絞られても、綺麗にする為石に叩きつけられても、それでも我等は神の臨在の栄光の前に立つ価値も無く、立つ事が出来ません。

　更に我等は自分が磨いた総ての壷を見せても、自分が行った総ての善行を示しても、自分自身を神に受け入れらる者となす事は出来ません。「正しい業もすべて汚れた着物のようになった、」（イザヤ　64：5）我等の唯一の望みはキリストの下に行き、我等の状態を告白して、救いの着物を着せて頂くしか道はありません。その時初めて神の光に曝され、霊の微風を楽しむ事が出来ます。

祈祷：　聖なる神よ、私はあなたに私の罪を告白します。御子イエス・キリストを通してのみ与えられる救いの着物を着せて、私を清めて下さい。

The Lamb's Book of Life[li]

The city does not need the sun or the moon to shine on it, for the glory of God gives it light, and the Lamb is its lamp ... Nothing impure will ever enter it, nor will anyone who does what is shameful or deceitful, but only those whose names are written in the Lamb's book of life.
~ Revelation 21: 23, 27 (NIV).

A few years ago my alma mater asked its graduates to contribute to the rebuilding of the campus center and to do this by buying a brick in the pathway that leads to that building. The bricks were to be engraved with the names of the alumni donors, but this seemed to me a terribly vainglorious way to contribute and I did not participate.

This fall when I visited the campus and recognized the names of former classmates on the walkway, I felt disappointed that more of my old friends were not represented there. So I did an "about face" and bought a brick. Not only will my name be engraved, but also a reference to today's Scripture passage.

While I was a freshman at this Christian college, I first heard there was a *Lamb's Book of Life*. (Before then, all I knew about was the other book – that great book to be opened on Judgment Day and read to all mankind, the book where every sinful thought, word, or deed I'd done had been recorded.) I can't describe the joy, the relief, the thanksgiving in my heart to discover there was another book, and so I came to Jesus and found in him forgiveness and peace.

As I go through life, I write my name someplace, or for somebody, almost every day, but this life passes away, and in time, even my name on a brick at the campus center will be worn away, decayed by the elements. The only lasting record of my name is in the *Lamb's Book of Life*. Knowing that brings me peace, for I am assured eternity with the Lord in that glorious city of God.

Prayer: Heavenly Father, I'll need eternity to fully express my gratitude. Thank you; in Jesus' name. Amen

Light for the Lost[lii]

And God said, "Let there be light," and there was light. ~ Genesis 1:3 (NIV)

Every good and perfect gift is from above, coming down from the Father of the heavenly lights, who does not change like shifting shadows. ~ James 1:17 (NIV)

When my sister was little, she awoke one night, and tried to find our mother in the darkness. The family had just moved to a new house and she was frightened. She groped along to what she thought would be the hallway but walked into a corner. Frustrated, she began to cry.

Mother came and peering into the bedroom called, "Dorothy, where are you?"

A small voice sobbed, "I don't know. I'm lost."

Mom turned on the light, and Dorothy ran into her arms – safe at last.

What a picture of our common human experience! We come into the world as strangers to a new home. We struggle to get our bearings – groping, stumbling, calling out from the darkness, "I'm lost." Who will turn on the light and show us the way?

From the moment He said, "Let there be light," God has been our loving parent. He brightens the dark world, provides a lamp for our pathways, and sent Jesus, who promised, "Whoever follows me will never walk in darkness, but will have the light of life." (John 8:12b, NIV)

Be an Agent of Change
(A 50-word or less devotion on a question Jesus asked)

Question: *"You are the salt of the earth. But if the salt loses its saltiness, how can it be made salty again?..."* ~ Matthew 5:13 (NIV)

Devotion: Without our Lord's intervention, the world would run amuck. If no one heeded the call to repent, to change, to forgive as forgiven, to render aid or seek peace, all existence would be evil and bleak. Through Christ's salvation, we're born anew and made seasoning for a world otherwise corrupt.

Storms of Temptation

Preparing for Snakes

Jesus told his disciples, "Situations that cause people to lose their faith are certain to arise. But how horrible it will be for the person who causes someone to lose his faith!" ~ Luke 17:1 (GW)

Old-time American entertainer W.C. Fields once said, "I always keep a supply of stimulant handy in case I see a snake – which I also keep handy." Clearly he wanted an excuse to use his "stimulant" – alcohol.

I, too, keep things around "in case" – extra cash in my wallet, sunglasses, a spare umbrella, a sweater in winter should the heat fail, in summer should the air conditioning be drafty. I carry saline solution should my contact lenses fog up, and spare keys should I lock myself out of the car. It's an endless list and all for the "snakes" I fear, a whole potful of anticipated calamities. In truth, I seldom use any of the stuff I tote around.

But like W. C. Fields, I do carry one thing that I actually hope to have to use – the high-calorie snacks I keep in case I should feel hungry. Ah, yes, the fear-of-hunger "snake." That's what enables me to enjoy my favorite indulgence.

My aunt once told me that when she is in a supermarket, she tries so hard not to buy ice cream. And when she gets it home she tries so hard not to eat it! (I guess certain weaknesses run in our family.)

It's difficult to not give into temptation however it might come into our path. But we are foolish to provide the temptation to ourselves.

Prayer: Forgive me, Lord, for being weak when faced with temptation. Embolden me to be as strong as a bear; in Jesus' name. Amen

***

Danger!
Don't flirt with temptation.[liii]

Can a man scoop a flame into his lap and not have his clothes catch on fire? ~ Proverbs 6:27 (NLT)

Occupy your day with worthy pursuits, and the Tempter will work on someone who's not quite so busy.

***

Train Ride
Don't hook your caboose to just any engine.[liv]

My child, if sinners entice you, turn your back on them! ~ Proverbs 1:10 (NLT)

The world is full of many who would pull you off track. Before you embark, find out where the train is headed.

Nighttime of Trust and Peace

Matthew 6:25-34 (NLT)

"That is why I tell you not to worry about everyday life — whether you have enough food and drink, or enough clothes to wear. Isn't life more than food, and your body more than clothing? Look at the birds. They don't plant or harvest or store food in barns, for your heavenly Father feeds them. And aren't you far more valuable to him than they are? Can all your worries add a single moment to your life?

"And why worry about your clothing? Look at the lilies of the field and how they grow. They don't work or make their clothing, yet Solomon in all his glory was not dressed as beautifully as they are. And if God cares so wonderfully for wildflowers that are here today and thrown into the fire tomorrow, he will certainly care for you. Why do you have so little faith?

"So don't worry about these things, saying, "What will we eat? What will we drink? What will we wear? These things dominate the thoughts of unbelievers, but your heavenly Father already knows all your needs. Seek the Kingdom of God above all else, and live righteously, and he will give you everything you need.

"So don't worry about tomorrow, for tomorrow will bring its own worries. Today's trouble is enough for today."

Don't Borrow Trouble[lv]

Therefore do not worry about tomorrow, for tomorrow will worry about itself. Each day has enough trouble of its own. ~ Matthew 6:34 (NIV)

As a child, I lived in perpetual dread of things that might happen. At times I felt paralyzed by my fear. In an effort to help, my mother showed me today's passage from the "Sermon on the Mount."

"To follow Christ's teaching means learning not to borrow trouble from the future," she said. "Instead of anticipating all possible calamities, focus only on the day at hand." When I tried this, I found it reduced my number of worries significantly.

As an adult, I know the passage has broader application than simply reducing anxiety. Jesus' teaching reveals that as each day brings its concerns and responsibilities, we are to consider daily what the Lord has for us to do. Then we must do it, day by day.

Prayer: O Lord, help me to trust all my tomorrows to your keeping and to work at what you would have me do today; in Jesus' name. Amen

Ruth 2:17-22 (GW)

So Ruth gathered grain in the field until evening. Then she separated the grain from its husks. She had about half a bushel of barley. She picked it up and went into the town, and her mother-in-law saw what she had gathered. Ruth also took out what she had left over from lunch and gave it to Naomi.

Her mother-in-law asked her, "Where did you gather grain today? Just where did you work? May the man who paid attention to you be blessed."

So Ruth told her mother-in-law about the person with whom she worked. She said, "The man I worked with today is named Boaz."

Naomi said to her daughter-in-law, "May the LORD bless him. The LORD hasn't stopped being kind to people – living or dead." Then Naomi told her, "That man is a relative of ours. He is a close relative, one of those responsible for taking care of us."

Ruth, who was from Moab, told her, "He also said to me, 'Stay with my younger workers until they have finished the harvest.'"

Naomi told her daughter-in-law Ruth, "It's a good idea, my daughter, that you go out to the fields with his young women. If you go to someone else's field, you may be molested."

No Matter Where[lvi]

...Where hast thou gleaned to day? ~ Ruth 2:19 (KJV)

I recently left my job because of disturbing events (a change in management and policy) that I did not understand and over which I had no control. When friends asked, "Have you found work?" I would respond, "No, I'm still unemployed."

After prayer, however, I realized I'm not unemployed, just unsalaried. I'm learning new computer software, running errands for the elderly, catching up around the house, and doing more reading and writing. The Lord has given me new assignments, and I'm learning to trust that he will bless my efforts and open new doors. When the Lord asks, "Where hast thou gleaned today?" I want to have a good reply. The "where" has changed from a skyscraper in lower Manhattan to my own home and the new computer on my kitchen table. But no matter where, I pray that my work is pleasing to God and in a field that produces much fruit.

Prayer: Heavenly Father, lead me to the work you would have me do each day; in Jesus' name. Amen

Exodus 14:21-22 (NIV)

Then Moses stretched out his hand over the sea, and all that night the LORD drove the sea back with a strong east wind and turned it into dry land. The waters were divided, and the Israelites went through the sea on dry ground, with a wall of water on their right and on their left.

Deep Waters[lvii]

"Take my yoke upon you, and learn from me, for I am gentle and humble in heart, and you will find rest for your souls. For my yoke is easy, and my burden is light." ~ Matthew 11:29-30 (NIV)

My friend Karen recently told me she'd taken a two-hour canoe trip. Her news surprised me because she cannot swim and has always avoided water sports. "You know why I did it?" she asked, "because the water was only knee high!" We both laughed and I congratulated her.

Karen conquered her fear by taking a "baby step" and doing only as much as she felt she could handle. Her little canoe adventure reminded me how Jesus helps us to grow in faith, one learning experience at a time.

Everyone has his or her own personal "deep waters" that cause fear and trepidation. But the Lord calls us to trust in him and promises to equip us for life's challenges. As we daily walk with Jesus and ask for his help with every "baby step" we take, we learn we can lean on him more and more. We grow in faith that Jesus will not allow the deep waters we dread to overwhelm us.

Prayer: Dear Lord, thank you for your promise to walk with us day by day – and to always hold us in the palm of your hand. Amen

Psalm 111 (GW)

Hallelujah!
I will give thanks to the LORD with all my heart
   in the company of decent people and in the congregation.
The LORD's deeds are spectacular.
   They should be studied by all who enjoy them.
His work is glorious and majestic.
His righteousness continues forever.
He has made his miracles unforgettable.
   The LORD is merciful and compassionate.
He provides food for those who fear him.
He always remembers his promise.
He has revealed the power of his works to his people
   by giving them the lands of other nations as an inheritance.
His works are done with truth and justice.
   All his guiding principles are trustworthy.
     They last forever and ever.
     They are carried out with truth and decency.
He has sent salvation to his people.
He has ordered that his promise should continue forever.
   His name is holy and terrifying.
The fear of the LORD is the beginning of wisdom.
Good sense is shown by everyone who follows God's guiding
   principles.
His praise continues forever.

Beauty in the Darkest Sky[lviii]

The people walking in darkness have seen a great light; on those living in the land of the shadow of death a light has dawned. ~ Isaiah 9:2 (NIV)

So much of my time is spent in Manhattan that when I can, I drive upstate to the mountains. When I'm far away from all the city's artificial lights, I enjoy gazing into the nighttime skies and pondering the moon, the stars, and when conditions are right, even a distant planet.

Recently I have been troubled by a friend's illness and after spending time in prayer one morning, I sat back, closed my eyes, and thought about those cool, crisp summer evenings in the Adirondacks. It's there that I can look up into the far reaches of the sparkling sky and behold God's power in its silent and glorious display.

The panorama reminds me that God is in control and will give each of us the grace we need in trying times. For as we live the days of our lives, there surely will be some nights that are dark with difficulty. When we get away from the artificial lights of this world – the things of earth which clamor for our attention – we can focus on God's undimmed power and love, just like the stars that shine brightest in the darkest sky.

Prayer: Heavenly Father, we thank you for creating beauty in the universe and for the message of power and love displayed in the starry skies. Be with us as we walk through times of darkness and help us to keep our focus on the light that is Jesus Christ; it's in his name we pray. Amen

Sure Steps[lix]

A man's steps are directed by the LORD. How then can anyone understand his own way? ~ Proverbs 20:24 (NIV)

When my employer announced plans to relocate, I started a job hunt right away. Seeing my haste, a friend cautioned me to pray. "Pray first. Then take steps," he advised, "and trust God to bring your foot down in the right place."

So before mailing out more resumes, I paused and asked the Lord to direct me and to ensure my foot landed in the right job. Then I got busy lining up interviews.

One day, quite unexpectedly, the supervisor of another department offered me a promotion. She explained that only one division was relocating out of state, not the whole corporation. She apologized that the new job would not be a part of the move!

She had mistakenly thought I wished to relocate. And I had mistakenly thought that my only option was to seek employment with another firm. How thankful I felt when I learned the truth. Even though I had stepped out in the wrong direction, the Lord heard my prayer and turned me around. The Psalmist is right. We don't always understand the way we should take, but when we trust the Lord, he directs our steps.

Prayer: Lead me, Lord, for you know the way better than I, and your plans far exceed my own; in Jesus' name. Amen

***

Handling Anger[lx]

In your anger do not sin: Do not let the sun go down while you are still angry, and do not give the devil a foothold. ~ Ephesians 4:26, 27 (NIV)

Be careful – the problem with anger is what you do with it. Before you react in anger, consider this: Did you hear what the other person meant, or did you hear what you would have meant, had you spoken the words?

Sometimes It's Best Not to Listen!

Do not let any unwholesome talk come out of your mouths, but only what is helpful for building others up according to their needs, that it may benefit those who listen. ~ Ephesians 4:29 (NIV)

I visited my 98-year-old aunt recently. She lives in a lovely continuing-care facility and receives lots of love and attention. All of the 18 residents are elderly and have sweet personalities, but at times they can become confused.

I sat with my aunt in the dining room and watched as one-by-one, others were brought to their tables for lunch. Madge, whose mind sometimes wanders from reality, was helped to her place and then in a loud voice called out, "Well, isn't someone going to call the police?"

Jill, an employee at the facility, asked, "Why?" and Madge snapped back, "Because of the intruders!"

Jill knew there hadn't been any break-ins and started to contradict her. When Madge became more agitated, Jill tried to calm her down by taking a new approach. "Oh, we took care of them," she said, dismissing the subject with a wave of her hand. I saw Madge relax.

But a second resident, seated at a different table, overheard and asked her friends, "What did she say? Who did they take care of?" and her table companion replied, "The intruders."

A third resident, seated at a third table, overheard that remark and piped up with an anxious, "There were intruders?"

Soon everyone was upset and about something that hadn't even happened. (My aunt's hearing aid was missing so she alone remained calm.)

The moral of my story: Not everything we hear is true. We do well to remember these words: *Thou wilt keep* him *in perfect peace, whose mind* is *stayed* on thee*: because he trusteth in thee.* ~ Isaiah 26:3 (KJV)

Prayer: Heavenly Father, our most gracious caregiver, protect us from false teaching and rumors. Keep our hearts and minds focused on your truth; in Jesus' name. Amen

Relinquishing My Will

The LORD is like a father to his children, tender and compassionate to those who fear him. For he knows how weak we are; he remembers we are only dust. ~ Psalm 103:13-14 (NLT)

When I was a child I trembled at the thought of relinquishing myself to God's leading. I'd learned about all the heroes in the Bible and the tremendous tests they were put to in keeping their faith.

Noah had to bounce along at the whim of the waves not knowing when or where his travels would end. Daniel had to face the lions, trapped with them in a den overnight. Shadrach, Meshach, and Abednego were thrown into a fiery furnace. The list went on and on – Samson, Ruth, Rahab, David, and Mary, the mother of Jesus – all served the Lord by submitting their wills to his.

I felt timid. Who was I to take on such challenges? Isn't it easier to be a weakling and continually petition the Lord for his forgiveness?

Today's verse tells us that our Heavenly Father is kind to his children. It makes me think about my earthly father and how he often challenged me. He taught me how to ride a bike, encouraged me to learn to play a musical instrument, and brought me to Sunday school and church.

Each new experience was a challenge at the time, even some things that I thought I'd never be able to handle. But I trusted that with my parents' help, my loving parents' help, new tasks could be mastered no matter how formidable they seemed at first. And the rewards promised were life changing.

I love life and want to continue to live, to protect myself from harm. Though I sometimes fear that God's challenges will be dangerous, peace comes when I recall that the Lord and I have the *ultimate* of father-child relationships. God loves me more than anyone. I need not fear.

Prayer: Heavenly Father, thank you for your kindness and for watching over me with love; in Jesus' name. Amen

Clear Skies of Thankfulness

Daily Guideposts Reader's Room: A Helping Hand[lxi]

How has God been reaching out to me this year? With His all-powerful hand!

In January, I fell on the ice and broke my wrist – my first experience with broken bones. After nine weeks, I am out of the cast and have completed two weeks of physical therapy.

I am so thankful every time I master a new task. At first, I rejoiced before the Lord every time I buttoned a button, turned a knob or signed my name. Now I thank Him that I can type with both hands and play the piano again. I also thank him for the ability to wash the dishes, vacuum the floors, make the beds and cook dinner. I thank Him that I can turn a key in a lock and open a door.

I also thank Him for what I see others doing. When I attended a symphony orchestra concert this weekend, I studied the musicians and marveled at everything the human hand can do. And I marvel at the hand of God knitting my bones back together when they were hidden in the cocoon of a cast.

Helene C. Kuoni, Basking Ridge, New Jersey

Baby's First Word

So then, just as you received Christ Jesus as Lord, continue to live in him, rooted and built up in him, strengthened in the faith as you were taught, and overflowing with thankfulness. ~ Colossians 2:6-7 (NIV)

Had a nice chat with my friend Annemarie who visited from Germany. She brought me up to date on everyone in her family back home, and ended with a report on her youngest granddaughter, Ella.

"What do you think was Ella's first word?" Annemarie asked. Then, without waiting for me to respond, she added: "It was 'danke' (thank you). She didn't say 'Mama' or 'Papa,' but 'thank you!'" Annemarie laughed with delight as she told me.

I laughed too. Little Ella was the most grateful baby I'd ever heard of!

Certainly her parents must be very polite and appreciative people. How else, except from hearing them say "danke" to each other repeatedly, could little Ella have learned that word? I thought it was wonderful. The baby, by mimicking her parents, learned from her first word on, to express an appreciative heart.

Danke, Ella, for reminding me of the word that should always be first on my lips.

Prayer: Thank you, Lord. My heart is overflowing with thankfulness for your love, your mercy, your kindness to me; in Jesus' name. Amen

Trails to Travel

Traveling Light

These were his instructions: "Take nothing for the journey except a staff – no bread, no bag, no money in your belts." ~ Mark 6:8 (NIV)

Taste and see that the LORD is good. Oh, the joys of those who take refuge in him! Fear the LORD, you his godly people, for those who fear him will have all they need. Even strong young lions sometimes go hungry, but those who trust in the LORD will lack no good thing. ~ Psalm 34:8-10 (NLT)

I took a trip to Europe with my sister Marilyn, and was determined to travel light. I packed only one bag because I figured I'd see new places and meet new people every couple of days. It wouldn't matter if I kept wearing the same clothes again and again. My goal was to carry a light suitcase.

My sister packed two suitcases and acquired all kinds of souvenirs as we travelled along. Know what? With only one bag of my own to tote, I wound up helping Marilyn carry hers. Somehow my plan to travel light backfired. Not only that, but I see myself wearing the same clothes in all my vacation pictures.

Jesus instructed the disciples to take nothing for the journey except a staff. No food. No luggage. No money. All they were to take with them, for support and protection, was a staff – a piece of a small tree limb. Once again, Jesus' directions were new and radical! But one thing is sure. His teachings always point his disciples to a loving, heavenly Father and this occasion was no exception. Our God, who met the disciples' every need, will do the same for us as we travel through life with him.

Prayer: Jesus, you tell us you'll share our burdens. Help us to likewise share the burdens of our brothers and sisters, that they too might learn to lean on your love; in your holy name. Amen

Gotland – Top and Center[lxii]
(Newspaper Feature Article)

The wall across from my desk at work is covered end to end with "Philips' New Commercial Map of THE WORLD." And when I glance up from my figures, I confront two curiosities. The map, though it portrays such lands as Burma, Persia and the Belgian Congo, will always be "new" for by its title that is what it professes to be. Secondly, it was produced in London and the British mapmakers chose to place Europe, Scandinavia and Africa in the center of the world. India and Asia to the South Pacific are presented on the right and the Americas appear on the left.

It is somewhat distressing to see one's homeland portrayed off-center, for from earliest school days, the United States has been the hub of the world for me. But the hours I have spent with this map have had their subtle influence and this summer when my sister Marilyn and I traveled to Sweden, I felt it was a journey to the land Philips presents "top and center."

We arrived late in July and after a mini-tour of Stockholm with our gracious host and musical colleague, Gunnar Melin and a fun excursion through the Vasa Museum with Salvation Army's own Gurli Johnson, we boarded a Linjeflyg jet for the island of Gotland, that incomparable limestone plateau, 56 miles offshore in the Baltic.

Gotland was the focal point of our three-week itinerary because it was there that my grandmother was born many years ago. It was there, cradled in her mother's arms, she was brought to the 14th century church at

Martebo to be baptized and there that she skipped and ran through the rose-bordered pathways of her childhood home. As a young woman she brought the gentle, graciousness of her early days to a new home in America where she married and gave birth to her daughter, who gave birth to me. This summer, the Gotland I had learned of so long ago became suddenly, magically, real and alive.

We were met by our second cousin's wife, Maria, whose warm "welcome" was the first bud of spring and suddenly just as a meadow may blossom overnight, we were deep in the fragrance of friendship and family. To us, who can count our American relatives on one hand, the procession seemed endless – Rolf and Kristina, Karin and Georg, Sten-Eric, Leif, Tomas, Birgit, Anette, Signe, Fanny, Veda, ad infinitum – as endless as the coffee they poured, the variety of cakes that we ate.

How quickly they made us feel at home in this "top and center" part of the world – a world of centuries-old stone houses, featherbeds and lace curtains, oak storage chests, candles and crystal chandeliers.

Maria was our guide through this island wonderland of tradition and beauty and as we walked the narrow, cobblestone byways of Visby and around its medieval stone wall, she shared Gotland's history and legend.

She told us of the Danish king, Valdemar Atterdag who invaded the city and of the brutal punishment of the young girl who betrayed her people to help him. We learned of Norwegian King Olof who brought Christianity with the help of his army – how he fell to his knees imploring God's help for the victory and how marks of his elbows and knees are impressed on the stone to which he fell.

On the Baltic West Coast she told us the legend of Licker Snälle and the rock formation which is called Jungfrun. As we walked a pre-historic labyrinth and drove through prize-winning meadows, she shared stories of some detail.

"Those two stones," she pointed out, "used to be women" and we learned of their punishment for quarreling one Sunday morning as they walked to church.

"And those two stones used to be bulls!" and we learned of the selfish farmer whose son was healed of his blindness, but who withheld the animals he was to present to God in thanksgiving.

This summer we were part of my grandmother's world. We were part of an idyllic blend of the present with all the generations before us. A world of old family portraits, of tombstones and cobblestones. A world of centuries-old churches built for a future even longer than their past. But it is the people, a people of warmth, hospitality and grace, who make this without reservation, a "top and center" part of the world.

Dalarna First[lxiii]
(Newspaper Feature Article)

When I was a little girl and unfamiliar with Swedish traditions and trinkets, a young engineering student from Stockholm visited one Sunday. After dinner my father suggested a tour of local historic sites, but Åke preferred a trip to the basement to see our washing machine.

"How odd, these Swedes" I thought, attributing his tastes to nationality instead of occupation. Even more fascinating was the curious remembrance he left with my mother – a small, red horse he said came from Dalarna.

It was made from the tiniest block of wood but each year as I grew to know and love the culture of my forebearers, that little Dalahäst seemed to swell to greater dimensions. When my sister, Marilyn, and I traveled to Sweden this summer we wanted to see Dalarna first.

We rented an auto in Stockholm and after a night's rest to keep jet lag at bay, we started our drive northwest through forest, farmland and meadow. With blissful abandon we drove further and further from Stockholm never anticipating the mulish nature of our car. But after lunching at a roadside table in Avesta, the cantankerous compact stubbornly refused to leave its idyllic surroundings.

My heart pounded as I searched for the operator's manual and ached when I found it – written in Swedish!

"Not to worry" my sister tried to reassure me. "Didn't I have two terms of Swedish conversation?"

I doubted her "Jag heter Marilyn. Vad heter du?" could save the day. But we scanned the manual until we found "Trampa ned kopplingspedalen" and decided that could only mean, "Tramp on the clutch pedal." Though it is unlikely Berlitz would endorse our translation, the car understood and soon we were back in the flow of traffic.

Traveling through long colonnades of tall pines, Route 70 took us from one cluster of wooden houses to the next. Every house had a tile roof and a nearby pile of logs, cut and stacked for the winter. Without variation the houses were painted a rich, deep red. And each hamlet had its complement of sheep, cattle and chickens.

We had heard that "three out of every two" men from Dalarna, play the violin. So it was only natural, I suppose, that our first acquaintance in Tällberg should be a fiddler. A hearty octogenarian, he and two other musicians provided the evening's entertainment and the patio at Tällbergsgården was crowded with dancing guests. We joined the party for its procession to the front lawn where the innkeeper's wife stood at the flagpole, dressed in the colorful costume of the province. Her long sleeves billowed with the evening's breeze as the flag was lowered into her arms. The sun was setting over Lake Siljan and the innkeeper raised his näver horn for a mellow *Taps*. What possibly could follow such a moment of peace, contentment, tranquility?

Only a pot of strong coffee, that's what!

I had no place to rest my cup until my fiddlin' friend beckoned me to his table and set the stage for an evening of conversational pantomime. It took time but we communicated and after a half hour of charades I knew he had sailed to the United States in 1956. He traveled with his violin and played in New York, Chicago and Kansas City. With singleness of purpose he spent the rest of the evening conjuring up the names of other locations – Minneapolis, St. Paul, Duluth.

Meanwhile, the hotel proprietor, a gracious emcee, decided his guests would enjoy an interview with my sister. In his native tongue he asked where she was from, how long she would be in the country, and how she had descended from Swedes. When she replied in turn, "United States, tre veckor, mormor" he continued his questioning along those lines. I was awed by her performance and with a twinkle in his eye, my musician friend leaned across the table and whispered, "Detroit, San Francisco."

It was a fine trip through Dalarna, from Leksand to Rättvik to Mora – meeting those who lived there, touring the old stone churches and enjoying footpaths in the woods. We saw old log cabins with roof tiles anchored by heavy stones and Springkällan, a natural spring in the middle of the forest. We visited the Anders Zorn Museum and walked pedestrian shopping streets where the wooden horses of various sizes were raffled for charity. And finally, in Nusnäs we found the birthplace of thousands of painted horses just like the one Åke brought to New York so many years ago.

Yes, Dalahästar, I must tell you. We saw your homeland first and know what is there. You are right to stand proud.

Cruising the Göta Canal[lxiv]
(Newspaper Feature Article)

We Americans are known to plan European vacations that cover the *most* territory in the *least* number of days.

It is expensive to cross the Atlantic and we never know when we will have opportunity to do it again. Every trip must include as much as possible. Often stops on our marathon treks, allow only enough time for a click of the shutter so when we return home, we can view our slides and sigh, "I still can't believe I was there."

When my sister, Marilyn and I traveled to Sweden last summer, I confess our trip was largely the typical, American-style, madcap vacation. But in the middle of our three weeks we enjoyed three days of total relaxation. We took an idyllic, wonderland cruise on Sweden's scenic waterway, the Göta Canal.

We boarded the "Diana" at Riddarholmen just across from Stockholm's landmark Town Hall. With a total of 26 passengers on a craft built for 73, we had our choice of deck chairs and railing positions throughout the voyage.

It rained lightly that first day but we dined contentedly on tasty fish, chicken and rice, meatballs and muscles and settled in to enjoy our slow cruise through the lovely Baltic archipelago. Between grey skies and calm, colorless waters, we glided past thousands of silent, rock islands, each with its complement of spindly pine trees – an ethereal vision of beauty in the fine mist.

"Diana" was darling – only 29 meters long and less than seven meters wide. Our cabin was pint-sized, with barely room for two narrow cots and the tiniest sink in between. When I began to wash that evening,

Marilyn stretched out for a doze. Her pillow was next to the basin at about six inches less altitude. I felt silly washing my face looking down at a face looking up. Marilyn said it was an experience taking a nap and a shower at the same time.

We slept well and were awakened at 4 A.M. for the series of 15 locks at Berg. We should have stipulated "weather permitting" when we requested the pre-dawn reveille, for overnight we had been dealt a double dose of dense fog. As we heard the water rushing into each lock, we were blindly lifted from step to step, smelling the dew but unable to see the grassy shore, inches away. And the fog, unpleasant as it was, was only harbinger of the storm to come.

When we disembarked at Vadstena, the windows of heaven opened wide and our tour of the fortress-like castle, St. Brigit's Monastery, and the city's famous lace shops, had us darting in and out of the downpour. We longed to be back on board – dry, warm and squirreled away in our cabin napping.

Midway through the three-day excursion, the weather changed. We reached the Karlsborg lock where the sun shone brightly, not only from above but on shore from a cluster of five beaming faces – two men and three women blending their clear, strong voices and singing "Han ska öppna pärleporten" (*He the Pearly Gates Will Open*). Just as the water lifted the "Diana" from lock to lock, our spirits were elevated by the hymns they sang. The village folk stretched out their arms to our ship's rail and presented each passenger a bouquet of pansies and other flowers of the field.

We were to enjoy fair skies from that time on and had still to see magnificent Lake Vättern, the old locks at Trollhätten and the bustling Göteborg seaport, but the hymn-singing at Karlsborg was the highlight of it all for me. It ushered us into the very soul of the country, to the warmth and charm of the people and the beauty of nature all around. It lifted our thoughts from the fog and drizzle times of our lives and reminded us of our faith and our Father, creator of beauty and peace.

We cruised the Göta Canal and within our madcap, American-style marathon of a vacation, were blessed with three days that imbued the very spirit of the land.

NORDLEK '85 with Swedish Folk Dancers[lxv]
(Newspaper Feature Article)

There was dancing in a large tent, dancing in a gymnasium the size of a football field, in an ice palace, on open fields of grass, on bridges and barges, over hill and dale. It was NORDLEK '85, the convergence of 7,000 folk dancers from Sweden, Norway, Finland, Denmark, Iceland and the Faroe Islands. This year the Swedish Folk Dancers of New York were there too.

On Sunday, June 30, after a year of hard work, planning and practicing, dance leaders Yvonne Holland and Ron Hanson, President Dagny Crowley and 10 members of the New York club flew from JFK to Stockholm's Arlanda Airport. From there they flew to Helsinki via a smaller airplane and with an even smaller plane to Turku, the long dreamed about destination of the 16-hour journey.

Shortly after checking into the Rantasipi Ikituuri Hotel and meeting Elisabeth Krohn who had flown to Finland earlier, they were caught up in an exciting whirlwind of native costumes, flags and fiddles, food and friendship. Eva Nilsson from the Värmlands Föreningens Folkdanslag of Stockholm was their first new acquaintance. She introduced the New York contingent to her organization and together they marched to festivities at the Aura River. The crowd formed a circle so large it crossed two bridges and bordered both sides of the river. After the mayor's welcome, a barge bearing fiddlers and other musicians floated down the river filling the air with music, and suddenly the mile-wide circle of NORDLEK participants came to life with simple dances.

The official opening was later in the day at the Kuppis Ice Arena when 7,000 dancers in costume took part in the grand march, flags flying like opening day of the Olympics. There were speeches by representatives of each Scandinavian country and performances by several hundred Finnish dancers, an impressive show of talent, coordination, and grace.

In between NORDLEK's week-long schedule of events, our energetic "never-say-die" excursionists from New York bustled about on a city tour of Turku-Åbo, shopping sprees to Wiklunds Department Store on the main square, and a sightseeing bus and ferry tour through the islands of the Åboland Archipelago to Houtskär, where all sampled a local specialty, fish soup. They visited craft exhibits and at Domkyrkan heard a chamber music concert featuring Finland's national instrument, the kantele.

Charlie Erickson, Richard Haggblad, and George and Signy Ahlman even managed a Bastukväll (sauna) with the exhilarating regimen of repeated sprints from woodlands cabin to the chilly waters of a nearby inlet. After the sauna, in the setting midsummer sun, the club taught "Oh Susanna" and an early American mixer called "Bingo" to Swedes from the "National" dance group of Gothenburg and groups from Norway and Denmark. The National Folk Dancers later invited the New York club to perform with them at a nursing home – a heartwarming experience for our American group.

The week was quickly coming to an end on Saturday when 7,000 dancers paraded through town and out to a soccer field behind Samppalinna School. There each ethnic group performed separately. All reassembled later at the castle for the Hertig (Count) Johans banquet. A never-to-be-forgotten evening, dinner was just as it would have been in the 15th century – no forks and a round slice of thick, dark bread that served as a plate. But the affair was not without amenities. The count and his princess sang ballads, and diners were treated to songs on musical instruments of that period

Finally, the closing ceremony and the planting of a tree made NORDLEK '85 a memory. Some of the group, before hopping the Silja Line ferry to Sweden, rushed into town for last minute shopping and caught a glimpse of work crews dismantling the tents. Was it really over? Perhaps the physical structures were being lowered. But the spirit, the friendships, the new experiences would remain high in the heart till NORDLEK '88 in Norway. The Swedish Folk Dancers of New York plan to be there!

Dewdrops of Wisdom

Dorothy[lxvi]
(Essay)

So teach us *to number our days, that we may apply* our *hearts unto wisdom.* ~ Psalm 90:12 (KJV)

Dorothy could not take a walk in the woods without quoting Robert Frost, for sooner or later on our hike we'd find "two roads diverged in a yellow wood." She would stop in her tracks and recite the poem verbatim. As she spoke the lines, her expression and gestures became increasingly more dramatic. Finally, with voice raised and finger pointed to the sky, she'd intone the concluding lines with all the drama and emotion she could muster: "I took the road less traveled by and that has made all the difference."

Dorothy is no longer walking the yellow woods of this world, where crossroads demand decisions and where frustrating miles often separate us from our goals. She had many hopes and dreams, and so much more she'd wanted to accomplish. Along with her favorite poet, she might have thought she had "miles to go before I sleep."

But we do not determine the hour of our death, nor the time when our life's purpose is accomplished.

Dorothy traveled the miles allotted to her. She had her share of thrilling mountaintops and refreshing meadows. She walked some difficult terrain as well. She took every step with grace, with cheerfulness, and with her hand in our Lord's. She accomplished the miles He allowed, and today she is at rest.

When I think of her quick wit and her woodland recitations, I laugh; then I cry because I miss her. We like to believe we have miles to go before we sleep but that determination is God's alone. And so we must pray, "Lord, teach us to number our days that we too might apply our hearts unto wisdom."

The name Dorothy means "gift of God" and that she was! A gift to her many friends and co-workers. A gift to the churches where she played the organ. A gift to the choirs she directed. A precious sister to Thyra, Marilyn, and me. And to the family of God – a small branch of which was The Hollwegs Choir – a dear sister in Christ.

Growing Up[lxvii]

We do not wish for friends to feed and clothe our bodies – neighbors are kind enough for that – but to do the like office for our spirits. – Henry David Thoreau

After clothes shopping all day with my mom, we passed the jewelry counter and a sparkling ring caught my attention – a citrine surrounded by diamond chips. The salesman allowed me to try it on, but when he stated the price, I handed it back. Though I'd recently graduated from college, I still weighed expenditures like a "starving student." I spent money only when it was essential. Furthermore, I believed that jewelry should commemorate special occasions. This was just a shopping mall Saturday. My mother, who never spent money recklessly, surprised me. "You are working now," she said. "You have a good job. You can treat yourself, you know."

I looked at the ring. I wanted it, but still I hesitated, and Mom asked, "Why don't you buy it?"

"It's too good for me," I said.

The salesman overheard my remark and, banging his palm on the counter for emphasis, blurted, "Nothing is too good for you." He was a stranger, a salesman who wanted to sell, and yet his tone of voice told me more. Genuine and caring, his reaction exposed to me a serious problem – my low self-esteem.

I bought the ring and treasure it for many reasons, mostly for the memories of shopping with my mom, and for her wise counsel, but also for the memories of how the Lord used a stranger to change my life. I treasure it because on that day, many years ago, I caught a startling glimpse of myself and started to grow.

~

... Be honest in your evaluation of yourselves, measuring yourselves by the faith God has given us. ~ Romans 12:3 (NLT)

Thought ... Do you often compliment strangers? In a world that grows increasingly cold, when even families are distant, yours may be the only kind word someone receives and certainly needs.

***

Truth Telling[lxviii]

Always tell the truth but be diplomatic about it.

Let love and faithfulness never leave you; bind them around your neck, write them on the tablet of your heart. ~ Proverbs 3:3 (NIV)

You have no control over what the truth is, but you can control how you relay it. Use gentle words, and if the truth hurts, offer support and encouragement. Never forget that "truthful" and "kind" are meant to go hand-in-hand.

Picture It![lxix]

Life is the soul's nursery – its training place for the destinies of eternity.
– William Makepeace Thackeray

When my little fingers couldn't exercise any more, I'd put the violin down, and my mom would encourage me to keep practicing – *in my mind.* "Picture yourself fingering the notes in your head," she'd say. When I became discouraged with learning shorthand in high school, she'd say, "Practice the outlines in your mind while riding the bus to school." She offered the same advice for tennis and bowling: "Visualize! You don't have to be on the court or at the lanes in order to practice."

Mom's counsel was wise and followed the Lord's pattern, for didn't God *show* Abraham the stars and tell him to visualize the future? It's how Mom taught me about the Lord, too. She showed me His "picture" in the Bible, His "picture" in nature, and "picture" after "picture" of His working in people's lives.

Then one day, my turn came to return her advice. "When you're resting, Mom, close your eyes; picture your last physical therapy session. Master each technique in your mind. You'll walk again."

She nodded. She wanted to leave the hospital so badly and whispered, "I can picture myself walking home." "Good," I responded. "Visualize yourself using the hallway as an indoor track."

But Mom had meant something different and the next day, when she "walked" home to God, I realized that she'd been visualizing her walk into the arms of Jesus. Her whole life had been her preparation, her practice runway to Him. I treasure the wisdom she shared, and I can picture her on her walk home.

~

He took him outside and said, "Look up at the heavens and count the stars – if indeed you can count them." Then he said to him, "So shall your offspring be." ~ Genesis 15:5 (NIV)

Thought … Are your worldly burdens too heavy to bear? Focus on Heaven, the Christian's true home. In light of Heaven's glory, earthly troubles pale by comparison.

***

Godly Destination[lxx]

If you want to get somewhere, stay close to God

For the LORD watches over the path of the godly, but the path of the wicked leads to destruction. ~ Psalms 1:6 (NLT)

Begin with prayer, commit new endeavors to the Lord, take the steps that seem right and good, and keep the long view – it's not this earth that's the goal, but eternity.

Matthew 27:19-25 (NIV)

While Pilate was sitting on the judge's seat, his wife sent him this message: "Don't have anything to do with that innocent man, for I have suffered a great deal today in a dream because of him."

But the chief priests and the elders persuaded the crowd to ask for Barabbas and to have Jesus executed.

"Which of the two do you want me to release to you?" asked the governor. "Barabbas," they answered.

"What shall I do, then, with Jesus who is called Christ?" Pilate asked. They all answered, "Crucify him!"

"Why? What crime has he committed?" asked Pilate. But they shouted all the louder, "Crucify him!"

When Pilate saw that he was getting nowhere, but that instead an uproar was starting, he took water and washed his hands in front of the crowd. "I am innocent of this man's blood," he said. "It is your responsibility!"

All the people answered, "Let his blood be on us and on our children!"

Whose Way?[lxxi]

"What shall I do, then, with Jesus who is called Christ?" Pilate asked. They all answered, "Crucify him!" "Why? What crime has he committed?" asked Pilate. But they shouted all the louder, "Crucify him!" ~ Matthew 27:22-23 (NIV)

I once worked for a woman who delegated jobs with great flair but not much explanation. As a new employee, I didn't always understand what she wanted and would ask her to clarify. But instead of providing a little extra guidance, she acted annoyed, raised her voice, and repeated the assignment in the same unclear manner. She tried to intimidate me because she had a problem explaining herself clearly.

I thought of her when I read this morning's verses. It just seems to be human nature that when we don't know the specifics or can't explain our position on an issue, we shout louder. "Why? What crime has he committed?" Pilate asked. But the crowd had no answer, so they simply shouted louder to get their own way.

Shouting louder often works. But once we get our own way, is the Lord pleased? We should model our behavior after Christ, who said, "Not my will but thine be done." How much wiser to listen for God's truth rather than demand our own way!

Prayer: Lord, I need your wisdom to listen to others carefully – and to listen to you. Help me be more like Jesus. Amen

A Royal Education[lxxii]

When the queen of Sheba heard about the fame of Solomon and his relation to the name of the LORD, she came to test him with hard questions. Arriving at Jerusalem with a very great caravan – with camels carrying spices, large quantities of gold, and precious stones – she came to Solomon and talked with him about all that she had on her mind. ~ I Kings 10:1-2 (NIV)

Though she was royalty, and already in a position of power and prestige, the queen of Sheba desired something else: the wisdom she would need for a full and meaningful life. At great effort and expense "she came from the ends of the earth to listen to Solomon" (Matthew 12:42), and to learn about God – the source of Solomon's wisdom. She traveled many hundreds of miles by desert caravan to get from Sheba in southern Arabia to Israel's Jerusalem, and she brought countless chests filled with gold and precious gemstones to trade for her education.

College students today seek the best possible education they can afford, often stretching their resources to the limit or going into debt. Even so, college only prepares us for gainful employment; it cannot guarantee us a full or meaningful life. For that, we need wisdom.

The surprise God has in store for us is this: we can have the wisdom "fit for a king," for we, too, can study with Solomon! The instruction that cost the queen so much, is available to us when we open our Bibles to Proverbs, Song of Songs, Ecclesiastes, and Psalms 72 and 127 – all of which record Solomon's teachings. We do not have to embark on a long, arduous, and costly journey – we just need to ask the Lord to bless our "journey" into his Word.

Sensible people – young or old, rich or poor – are at their smartest when they seek the best education available, and at the same time, pursue the Lord's wisdom as taught by "Professor" Solomon.

Fighting[lxxiii]

If it's worth fighting for, try diplomacy first.

Do not quarrel with a person for no reason... ~ Proverbs 3:30 (GW)

Before engaging in battle, always consider the goal, the cost, the necessity, and the alternatives.

***

Setting Goals[lxxiv]

Set for yourself only lofty and noble goals.

Shoot for the moon, and even if you miss, you may fall among the stars. – Norman Vincent Peale

Failure is often an opportunity to set new goals. Try again and don't rest until your noble purpose is achieved.

***

Turn Off that Boombox[lxxv]

But the LORD was not in the wind. After the wind there was an earthquake, but the LORD was not in the earthquake. After the earthquake came a fire, but the LORD was not in the fire. And after the fire came a gentle whisper. ~ 1 Kings 19:11b, 12 (NIV)

Turn down your boombox if you want to hear God. If all you hear is the clamoring of the world, it's time to find a quiet place and listen for the voice of God. He speaks gently to your heart.

My Life Changed the Day I Got Stuck in the Elevator
(Essay)

When I was a little girl, my family frequently spent a Sunday afternoon visiting my great-aunt, Tante Annie, in Park Slope, Brooklyn, NY. Tante Annie and Onkel Fritz lived in a Victorian brownstone on 9th Street, and while my parents' generation lingered in the dining room over coffee, my two older sisters and I charged upstairs. There we could play "elevator" with the pocket doors that separated the hallway from the parlor.

The hallway, fairly narrow and bare, boasted a lush tapestry area-rug, and an ornate mirror that covered a three-foot wide section of wall and hung from ceiling to floor. The best feature of the hall, however, was the large, polished banister on the stairway. It tempted us to take a slide but we did not dare.

The parlor, on the other side of the doorway, contained interesting furniture including a heavy sideboard and elegant wing chairs. We gave the parlor the more prestigious role to play, that of the elevator.

We took turns operating the thick double doors of oak. Though heavy to push, they slid smoothly on their tracks until hidden in the walls on either side. They were magnificent doors, inlaid with frosted glass and etched with borders of flowers and foliage.

I could play the "operator" with aplomb, but as a lonely passenger waiting in the hall, I failed miserably. I would check my corkscrew curls and the ruffles on my Sunday dress in the mirror, but after that there was nothing left for me to do. One time it grew particularly tiresome and when I pressed the imaginary button on the wall, it was not in the spirit of a tinkling bell that I intoned the required "ding-a-ling." It was a demand and my anger smoldered inside. I pounded my fists and stomped my Mary Jane's. Soon my face was aflame. When the doors finally parted I shouted, "No fair. I'll be the elevator operator and make you wait. See how you like it."

We switched places, and while they waited in the hall, I closed the doors and began a revengeful perusal of every item in the sitting room. Sullenly, I fingered the scrolled arms of the loveseat and played with the crystal prisms that hung like fringe from the table lamp's dome shade. To confirm symmetry, I compared curlicues in each corner of the Oriental rug.

When I grew tired of pouting and decided the wait I had imposed on my sisters was sufficiently long to atone for their "sins," I parted the doors. They were gone.

I found them down in the kitchen eating ice cream.

My life changed the day I got stuck in the elevator. While the experience instilled an enduring appreciation for the details of Victorian furnishings, I also learned an important lesson for life: to imagine offense and seek revenge is to suffer loss in the end.

Gardens of Grace

Serving with a Smile

The king's officials answered him, "Your servants are ready to do whatever our lord the king chooses." ~ 2 Samuel 15:15 (NIV)

So you are no longer a slave, but a son; and since you are a son, God has made you also an heir. ~ Galatians 4:7 (NIV)

One lazy summer day when a friend and I hung out together and chatted about a litany of philosophical topics, she asked, "How do you think it feels to have servants waiting to do your every bidding?"

"I know how it might feel," I replied, "because I've hired electricians, plumbers, painters, accounting help at tax time, and the neighbor's children to shovel my drive when it snows. In small ways, I do know what it's like to have others serve me."

I told her that my "servants" show up on time, always with lots of energy and enthusiasm. "I'm here to do the best job I can for you, Mrs. Kuoni. Whatever you ask me to do, I'm here to do it your way." My friend recognized my "tongue in cheek," and we shared a good laugh.

Unfortunately, when the roles are reversed, I too fail as a servant. I rush. I make mistakes. I am not always ready and willing to serve.

I especially can fall short in my service to God. Yet the Lord is the best of all possible employers. When I fail, he offers forgiveness and that changes everything.

I consider the Lord's goodness to me and see that I'm no longer a "hired hand" but his child. My burden is lifted and with joy I try again.

Prayer: Almighty God, thank you for being my Savior and Lord. How might I serve you today?

Crocuses and Grace[lxxvi]

Finally, all of you, live in harmony with one another; be sympathetic, love as brothers, be compassionate and humble. Do not repay evil with evil or insult with insult, but with blessing, because of this you were called so that you may inherit a blessing. ~ 1 Peter 3:8-9 (NIV)

My sister Thyra's next door neighbor, not normally a friendly person, stopped by one day to ask a favor. She had just learned that the previous owner of my sister's house had died. Could she, she asked, take a couple of Mr. Schmidt's crocuses as a remembrance of him?

My sister is not a very good gardener and the only flowers she has are those that Mr. Schmidt planted. Unfortunately, he did not plant very many in the ground. Most of his flowers were in hanging baskets and he had taken them with him when he moved. So Thyra asked her neighbor, "How many?" When the woman replied, "Two," she gave her permission.

Later in the day, Thyra checked her front yard and discovered her neighbor had dug up and taken more than a dozen plants. She telephoned to tell me and she was furious. "I feel like giving her a piece of my mind. She's taken half of the flowers in my front yard. The nerve!"

I had to agree. It certainly wasn't right, but now my sister had to decide what to do about it. She didn't want to create greater hard feelings. We both know the admonition in Scripture to live in peace with everyone as much as it is in our power to do so.

She decided not to say anything to her neighbor, but to ask the Lord to take away the bitterness she felt. How I admired her decision! The matter concerning her neighbor's behavior is small stuff. Very small indeed, compared to my sister's opportunity to grow in grace.

So this Lenten Season, let us remember the Lord's grace toward us in that "while we were still sinners, Christ died for us." (Romans 5:8, NIV) Let us likewise, forgive our neighbors' failings. "Let there be peace on earth and let it begin with me."

Whom will You Serve?

...enable your servants to speak your word with great boldness.
~ Acts 4:29 (NIV)

With the cease-fire ordered and the Führer nowhere to be found, the foot soldiers of the Third Reich began their surrender. Knowing that the war had ended, a soldier named Helmut jumped into the chilly waters of the Elbe River and swam to the opposite bank where the Americans were encamped. Recognizing his new status as a prisoner-of-war, Helmut chose to place himself under American rule – his decision made in the flash of a moment. Of all the Allied Forces, he believed the Americans would be the most humane. Thankful for the treatment he received, he later became an American citizen.

All people choose their own masters one way or the other. The Bible speaks of a straightforward choice with only two alternatives – God or the world. It is not a question of whether or not to serve. God *created* us to serve. The very word "human," routed in the Latin "humus," means soil, or dust of the earth, and is related to the Greek "diakonos" which means servant.

So Scripture links our humanity to servitude. "I *served* the Lord with all humility…" (Acts 20:19 NIV, Italics mine). And again: "For even the Son of Man did not come to be served, but to *serve*…" (Mark 10:45 NIV, Italics mine).

We find an especially revealing description of Christ's humanity and its link to servitude in Philippians 2:6-7 (NIV):

> "Who, being in very nature God, did not consider equality with God something to be grasped, but made himself nothing, taking the very nature of a *servant*, being made in *human* likeness." (Italics mine).

Like it or not, we humans are servants. God created us in his own divine image and gives us the gift of free choice – not the choice *whether* to serve but *whom* to serve.

As I jump into the sometimes chilly waters of a writer's life, I often see my own self-interests on one shore and the interests of the Lord on the other. I know if I swim toward God and put myself under his authority, he will reward my efforts handsomely, for *"Those who have served well gain an excellent standing and great assurance in their faith in Christ Jesus."* ~ 1 Timothy 3:13 (NIV)

God is a loving and kind master, assigning tasks appropriate to our abilities, and enabling us to accomplish what he asks. Surrendering myself to his rule, I'm made a citizen of heaven. With thanksgiving, I will write of his mercy; every page will sing his praises.

Lighten Up!
(Essay)

Joy is not in things; it is in us. – Wagner

Want to shed the "excess baggage" and enjoy more of life? I learned how and it didn't cost a dime.

It began with a story. Mother Teresa, famous missionary in Calcutta, once made a personal-appearance tour in America. One member of the host committee was so moved by her message, he bought an airline ticket and planned to follow her to every speaking engagement. Then he unexpectedly got to speak with her in person.

He told her his plan to follow her and hear all she had to say because he needed to find her peace and joy. She advised him to sell the ticket and give the money to the poor. He didn't need to listen to her any more. Forfeiting his airline ticket for the sake of the needy would bring him the peace and joy he desired.

Mother Teresa's wisdom came from Jesus. Many years ago, he advised, *"If you want to be perfect, go, sell your possessions and give to the poor, and you will have treasure in heaven..."* (Matthew 19:21, NIV).

I wondered if Jesus could be speaking to me. I was not rich, yet my home was bulging with possessions. And much of what I owned, I kept for the wrong reasons.

I had my *Brownie Handbook* since childhood, tassels from graduation caps, every term paper for which I'd received an "A,"... I was living in the past!

I had stacks of magazines to read "someday," clothes I'd hoped would fit again someday,... I was fantasizing!

I had old tax records, bank statements, and cancelled checks; things I should have tossed long ago. Avoidance? Denial? Laziness?

I'd kept inherited items because they had belonged to someone I loved. Did they bring me pleasure or was I holding onto my grief?

I had lots of things I never used. I had record albums but played my CDs. I was unrealistic!

I'd been too acquisitive, begun too many collections,... Had I substituted possessions for richness of spirit?

After taking a hard look at myself, I began shedding my "excess," by throwing it out, selling it, or putting treasured old pieces to creative new uses. I transferred recipe files, hobby notes, and rough drafts onto my computer and discarded the old, dilapidated shoe boxes that had previously stored them.

Best of all, I gave a lot away – to libraries, nursing homes, schools, supermarket collection bins, and church-run thrift shops. I'm sharing inherited mementoes and old photographs with family and friends. No more boxes of bric-a-brac in the attic; I'm opening up, sharing, making others happy.

My possessions had weighed me down. I find the more I give away, the more buoyant I feel. Sanity returns, with peace and joy! Oh yes, I must confess this: I've begun storing something new – treasures in heaven.

"Do not store up for yourselves treasures on earth, where moth and rust destroy, and where thieves break in and steal. But store up for yourselves treasures in heaven, where moth and rust do not destroy, and where thieves do not break in and steal. For where your treasure is, there your heart will be also." ~ Matthew 6:19-21 (NIV)

Miss Lungen's Legacy
(Essay)

Children's children are a crown to the aged... ~ Proverbs 17:6 (NIV)

When I was a child, my mother gave me two dollars and 50 cents every Friday afternoon. With that in hand, and my portfolio under arm, I walked to our neighborhood Presbyterian church where Miss Dorothy Lungen waited in the basement to give me a piano lesson.

Miss Lungen's appearance seemed to change according to the number of hours I had practiced for my lesson. When I was prepared, her bleached-blond curls were dazzling and I admired her painted lips and her warm, contralto voice. Her shiny bracelets and earrings made her the fanciest lady in my world. When I was ill-prepared, her six-foot frame loomed over me. The veins in her neck popped out and she'd boom in powerful tones, "COUNT! I SAID, COUNT! ONE, TWO, THREE. PU-LEEZE COUNT!" Her too-sweet perfume stuck in my throat. Her operatic volume assaulted my eardrums. I could not think, no less count. When would the hour end? When would I be out of there?

Years later, after I had grown and moved away, I telephoned Miss Lungen on impulse and she invited me to visit. We made a date and when the day arrived I approached her apartment wondering which countenance I'd find. She was in her eighties but when she opened the door I saw she had not lost her flair for style. Meticulously groomed, she obviously had spent hours preparing for my visit. She wore a frilly blouse with ruffled collar and cuff. Her face was made up but no longer in a theatrical way. She had allowed her thick blond curls to go natural, to become a beautiful crown of white.

Her apartment was decorated for Christmas. Always skillful at stretching her budget, she had fashioned a large paper ball from the previous year's cards and hung it with red ribbons in the foyer. Her drop-leaf table, complete with homemade ornaments, was set for a festive tea.

She used the walls for support as she moved about and announced she had graduated from using a walker. I noticed the thick sole on her right shoe, designed to equalize the length of her legs. She told me of bungled hip surgery and how several inches were lost in the "do-over" operation. I looked for bitterness in her eyes but found none.

"Listen, Hon, would you believe I'll be 88 in April?" she asked. "Physically I feel great – in spite of my short leg. It's hard to walk but when I think of what I put up with, how much sickness I had all my life, it's really remarkable. I never thought I'd get to be 88 and feel great at this age. God is good."

I recalled there had been times of illness in her life, but as a child, my knowledge of medical problems was limited to having my cavities filled by the dentist. I'd never comprehended the pain she suffered. It startled me to consider it now. I sat silent and she turned her attention to the tea brewing in a chipped porcelain pot. Her brother, Henry, had played cello on the ocean liners, and had years ago brought the tea set for her from Japan. She never had money for travel, but she shared the excitement of his trips through the detailed diaries he kept.

When "Henny" was in town between trips, his friend Bill would visit with his violin on quiet Sundays. Dorothy, Henny and Bill would play trios all afternoon. How she relished the memory of those lovely times as she spoke of them.

"Music does so much for your soul," she said. "Sometimes I think *What should I do with myself?* And I go to the piano and play. Music is a beautiful thing. Don't ever be so busy that you don't have time for music. And do those things you really want to do while you're young. Old age limits you."

As we visited, she shared her one regret; she'd never married or had children. I thought of the endless stream of pupils who came from all over Woodlawn Heights and paraded down the basement steps of the old Presbyterian church for piano lessons. All the while her heart ached for a child of her own!

Many of her students became prominent musicians, church organists, band and choir directors, ministers, and elementary school music teachers. Those she taught are now teaching others; her legacy continues to the second and third generation.

When I think of Miss Lungen's life and broad influence, I see that God did after all, provide her a very remarkable family. In her old age, she knew it too. When we stood at the doorway and hugged good-bye, she said, "I'm very proud of all my children."

Grant me, sound of body and of mind, to pass an old age lacking neither honor nor the lyre. – Horace

Moonglow of Childhood Memories

Dorothy, Thyra and Helene picking apples

Helene with second cousin "Johnny Boy"

Thyra holding Helene's hand on Woodlawn Heights "June Walk"

"336 E. 236 St." on July 4th

E. 236 St. house after a snowstorm

Christmas 1948 with Grandma

St. Mark's annual Sunday school excursion to Indian Point (later to Bear Mountain) on Hudson River Day Line steamer *Alexander Hamilton*

Moonglow of Childhood Memories 257

Dorothy, Thyra, Marilyn, and Helene on Circle Line boat ride around Manhattan Island

Helene (wearing poodle skirt) with P.S. 19 classmates

My Two

I had two grandmothers
(as most folks do),
But one of mine was pink
And the other one was blue.

My pink grandma was pretty,
Always wore a stylish hat,
I thought my blue grandma was crazy
And that, pretty much, was that.

The first came every Sunday
For coffee and for cake,
The second lived upstairs
But the journey could not make.

The first wore fancy, lacy gloves
And crocheted bag did carry,
The second suffered from old age,
In senility did tarry.

I learned a lot from both these two
As different as can be
Lessons for a lifetime,
They shared, in love, with me.

One showed me how a lady acts
Polite, demure and true
The other needed me to serve,
As our Savior taught us to.

Today, I thank the Lord for both,
A balanced pair they made
May my memories of their special gifts
Never, never fade.

Thanksgiving Day Parade
(Essay)

Every Thanksgiving Day, even before the sautéed onions, bread crumbs and celery were stuffed into the turkey, Mom filled brown paper bags with her homemade chocolate chip cookies. With the bags in hand, Dad led us kids out the front door. We ran down the steps with abandon and in our rush to be off to the big parade, hardly saw Mom's wave or heard her familiar admonition: "Be careful."

We started out early and took the bus to E. 205th St. where the Independent Subway Line began. We found the platform empty, and when the train pulled in found plenty of seats available. No rush-hour crush of business folk and office workers. It was a holiday, and being kids, we tried out all the seats. Then we whooped it up swinging around the gleaming floor-to-ceiling poles that on workdays provided balance for the swaying rush-hour passengers.

Thyra and Dorothy, being older than I, were taller. They stretched their arms up to hang onto the dangling leather straps, their sense of balance challenged every time the train took a curve. We found lots of excitement in all the clattering and squealing, and the irregular flickering of the lights. It proved the normal bumpy, jerky ride, but fun and novel to us, as the motorman sped us to Manhattan's Columbus Circle Station.

Once back up in the open air, we hiked to some street in the West 60s and claimed our "spot" on Central Park West. Over an hour before the parade would start, we found our prime viewing location right up against the wooden sawhorses. With our location claimed, next came the interminably long wait. After the exciting subway ride this non-activity, this standing and waiting, proved tedious. My feet got tired and my back yearned for a chair. Fidgeting, I ached to flee this awful confinement, my feet planted on a single spot of cold sidewalk for so long.

We didn't dare budge, however, or the assembling throng would crowd us out in a minute and the prized location we'd woken up so early, and traveled so far to win, would be lost forever. At a young age we New York kids learned how to "stand one's ground" in spite of intrusive elbows and shoulders, and strangers' pleas to pass through "just for a minute" or "just to take a picture." *Yeah, right!* We knew how to recognize a ruse.

We had a secret weapon to fortify us in this annual battle not to lose our "spots," not to succumb to the jostling crowd. It was Dad dolling out Mom's chocolate chip cookies that kept us content.

We sister-comrades also knew how to keep each other in line. After all, if any one of us lost our ground, the whole sisterhood would suffer the consequences. I remember Thyra periodically frowning, giving me a certain look that said "Beware." Her glance and the nod of her head in one direction or the other was code for "Helene, watch your left (or right) side. Someone's trying to inch their way in." We paid our dues for these spots and we understood our right to hold onto them.

Finally someone in the crowd would cuff their ear and say "Listen" and we'd hear the sound of muffled drumbeats wafting up the avenue. Instantaneously we were up on our toes, straining to see a parade not yet come into view. Gone was our juvenile impatience, our weariness. No longer did we fidget or whine of tired feet. The oncoming costumes, the music, the floats, the banners all captivated our attention, not to mention the huge helium-filled balloons that required hundreds of Macy's employees to guide and control. And the clowns were everywhere. I cringed every time one of those undisciplined jesters spotted us and made his way over. I never knew what high jinks to expect.

In 1951, the first time I was old enough to be included on this outing, Dorothy, a seasoned veteran of Macy's Thanksgiving Day parades, announced, "My favorite band is the *Philadelphia Mummers*. I can't wait to see them." Her pronouncement certainly caught my attention. Every band was terrific as it marched by. I couldn't imagine how one group might stand out from all the rest. But the name "Mummers" fascinated me. When they came into view and I heard the stringed-instrument sound of their banjos, violins and accordions, I looked up at Dorothy and said, "They're my favorite, too."

Such strange instruments for a marching band! But they produced a marvelous sound and the musicians put on a marvelous show. Their satin costumes were sequin-studded and they were bedecked all over with colorful plumes. The elaborate feathers made each man appear eight feet wide and they wore incredible headdresses that made them appear eight feet tall. They even walked their own special mummer's walk – a low, bent-knee strut and their choreography had them weaving back and forth like shuttles on a loom.

Each line of musicians wended its way through all the rest until it seemed they'd made a tangled mess of themselves. But they knew what they were doing and eventually found their way back into march formation. All the while they kept the music going: *Oh Dem Golden Slippers*. Thinking back today, I wonder what James A. Bland who wrote the music in 1879, would have thought to see his composition performed in such a flamboyant, fanciful spectacle as this. I doubt he could enjoy it more than Dorothy and I.

The best part of this parade was that we could watch without a care in the world. Only the wooden sawhorses stood between us and the action. And Dad stood behind us, watching over us and enjoying I'm sure, our little schoolgirl banter and gleeful clapping. We were oblivious to the possibility of pickpockets and other opportunists. Dad was there to keep us from harm. We were free to enjoy the fun and that was the reason he'd brought us. Yes, taking us out of the house meant our mother had full reign over the kitchen as she prepared Thanksgiving dinner. But the primary reason for taking us to the big parade was for us to have fun.

I know he enjoyed seeing our wonder as the Bullwinkle or Felix the Cat balloons passed overhead, when each elaborate float glided past, and each band marched by with their shiny brass horns blaring. We didn't like to see it all come to an end, our only solace, seeing Santa and his reindeer usher in the Christmas season.

Saint Patrick's Day Parade
(Essay)

The Thanksgiving Day parade was a thrill for Dad's children. We thought he was lucky to be at just about every New York City parade. But he was not there as a spectator. He was bass drummer for the Police Department Band and often marching proved to be hard work.

The first parade of the year was on St. Patrick's Day, March 17. In my dad's early band experience, the route up Fifth Avenue began at 44th Street and ended at 110th – the longest route of all *Big Apple* parades.

Over three miles of gleeful, ruddy-cheeked "sons of Erin" participated and put on a show that out-shined and out-distanced all other Irish festivities across America. Alfred Byrne, the Lord Mayor of Dublin, who sat in the 64th Street reviewing stand in 1935, commented that he'd never seen anything like it; nothing could compare in all of Ireland.

The 1935 event planners couldn't keep up with the number of people who wanted seats in the blocks-long reviewing stands. Parade committee chairman Roderick Kennedy told newspaper reporters, "I explain to the people asking for tickets that they won't get a seat anyway. But they insist so I give the tickets out to keep them quiet."

Every year spectators came in great waves and quarreled over seats, jostling for the best viewing locations. Then Patrolman Henry Quinn got things started, as he did every year. Standing at Fifth Avenue and 43rd Street, with whistle to his pursed lips, he blew a shrill blast, signaling the start of march. The units, lined up on the side streets, did not need to hear the signal twice. All were anxious to begin, and division after division stepped, in turn, onto the avenue.

The Ancient Order of Hibernians came first and was followed by contingent upon contingent of Knights of Columbus members, and Catholic university students – Fordham University, Manhattan College, St. Francis Xavier, and All Hallows. Many Holy Name Societies were represented, and green-kilted bagpipers, and Catholic high school bands from every borough. The perky majorettes, the baton twirlers, and the young musicians, proudly attired in uniforms of their school colors let loose with *Wearin' O' The Green* and *Irish Molly-O*. The glockenspiel players endlessly hammered out *The Bells of St. Mary* on their tinkling metal keys.

My dad saw the parade grow from 20,000 participants in 1930 to 95,000 in 1953, the last year the police department band participated. The spectators also grew in numbers. As early as 1938 when 50,000 marched, one million spectators were packed four to six persons deep on the sidewalks. Thick with O'Briens, Hogans, O'Connors, Tobins, and Gilhooleys, the crowd couldn't get enough and every year when folks returned, they brought along even more friends and family.

The day always began with a pontifical mass at St. Patrick's Cathedral. In 1939 the worshipping faithful thrilled to hear a cable read from the newly-elected Pope Pius XII. And Ireland sent a gift of 30,000 packages of shamrocks. Shamrocks, as every Irishman knew, memorialized St. Patrick's unique way of illustrating the Trinity – Father, Son, and Holy Spirit. That's also why the color of the day has to be green—green hats, scarves, coats, flags and banners, and streamers flung from the windows of office buildings at Rockefeller Center.

The St. Patrick's Day parade challenged everyone, not simply because of its length, but because it often took place in harsh winter weather. The event went forward as planned regardless of the temperature, rain, sleet, snow, or worst of all wind. Even in good years, when the sun gilded the houses of the east side of the avenue, and shined through the silk flags and banners, and put a gleam on brass trumpets and sousaphones, the wind still presented the real challenge. Whole contingents often marched with heads bowed to buck the offending gusts. At times the wind plastered the maroon and gold capes to the backs of the high school marchers. Streamers thrown from the windows soared and twisted in the breeze. Mighty gusts wrapped them around high tree limbs and traffic lights.

The high school students, who provided much of the music, were young and enthusiastic. So what if a downpour should drench them? They were invincible!

Those who marched with the patriotic and Irish societies were all ages. The three-mile trek may have been difficult. But their swinging arms were free of encumbrances and the sounds of a nearby band invigorated their gait. Furthermore they could take refuge on the sidelines any time they tired out.

The police and fire department band members, however, were neither teenagers nor empty-handed. They had no choice but to march on in the inclement conditions or frigid temps. Even the ground beneath their feet felt cold and the wind tore at their music. (Not only was St. Patrick's Day in winter, this parade followed the band season of Christmas programs and other indoor, sit-down concerts.)

Good thing my dad was strong. Born in 1903 he was in his thirties in the 1930s, in his forties in the 1940s, and 50 years old in 1953, the last time he marched on St. Patrick's Day. My dad didn't have the luxury of wheeling his big bass drum. He strapped it over the leather apron that protected his uniform and carried it the whole three miles, beating a strong march cadence most of the way. Good thing he had milestones by which to measure progress.

At 51st Street, the band passed *St. Patrick's* where Cardinal Hayes (and later Cardinal Spellman), stood waving to all from the massive doorway or on the cathedral's wide steps. What a picture he made in his scarlet robes, a biretta capping his head. Many leaders broke from the line of march to shake his hand or to genuflect. One could always count on seeing the clergy of St. Pat's. Archbishop Spellman's absence was conspicuous when he ministered to the battlefront troops overseas in 1943.

The war affected another long-standing tradition. The 165th National Guard Regiment, affectionately known as "The Fighting Irish" or "The Fighting 69th" was stationed in the Pacific war area in 1944. Their heartfelt radiogram to the parade committee proved they still participated in spirit. It read:

> "The regiment of today joins you over many miles in celebrating the feast of our beloved patron saint. On this occasion we reaffirm our devotion to his teachings, we rededicate ourselves to uphold the faith and aggressive traditions of our race and this regiment which has done much to make and keep America American."

The next milestone was the first of two reviewing stands. For many years, as surely as church officials could be found smiling and waving from the cathedral's steps, former New York Governor Alfred E. Smith could be found on the 64th Street reviewing stand. In the 1930s he'd be joined by Bronx Borough President Henry Bruckner and Mayor Walker. Later, when Fiorello La Guardia served as mayor, he'd also be at this location, as were Governor Dewey in the 1940s and Mayor Impellitteri in the early '50s.

The second reviewing stand stood another thirty-four blocks north at 100th Street. Though the day was growing dark, this third milestone meant only ten more blocks to go. The band began to play *Give My Regards to Broadway* and the high school baton twirlers began missing their catches. The police band's drum major Fred Ziegler somehow stood as tall and erect as ever. The musicians recycled their repertoire and tried to infuse *Garry Owen* with new vigor. The Fire Department band, not far behind, rang out with *McNamara's Band*.

On and on my dad's comrades marched with footfalls kept steady by the beat of his drum. At last they reached 110th Street and they could be relieved of their heavy instruments. How grateful they must have felt to pile them back in the band truck and see Jake Gumbel, who in his younger years had played French horn, drive them off to storage. It had been a long day. The boys could now join the other marchers in restaurants, bars and lunchrooms, wrap their chapped hands around warm mugs and gulp down hot coffee before heading home. Parade participants and spectators took off for dinners and balls at the city's various big hotels.

I remember believing that my father was a very strong man. I guess most children like to believe that about their fathers, but I wonder how many of my friends had dads, that in their fifties, could buck strong winds for three miles, ignore occasional downpours or snow squalls, all the while wearing a heavy woolen uniform, and carrying and beating a bass drum made of wood (fiberglass had not yet been invented). I guess that's why my dad slept soundly at night and why it was his habit to take every new pair of shoes to the shoemaker to be double-soled.

New York, a city of eight million, sees many ethnic parades – put on by the Greeks, the Poles, the Puerto Ricans, and the Norwegians to name just a few. Most had the good sense to have their national holidays fall in seasons of balmier weather.

Some years two parades fell on the same day and the police band would participate in one in the morning and the other in the afternoon. On one occasion the Police Band marched twice in the same parade. They headed the event in the parade's first division, marched the entire route, and piled their heavy instruments into the band truck. Then the men took the subway back to the parade's starting point at Battery Park. After a long wait, they retrieved their instruments and rejoined the line of march to bring up the rear. That was a challenge too, but I don't believe any other event taxed their stamina as did the parade to celebrate St. Patrick.

The Wellspring of Words
(Devotions for Writers)

News! News! A Birth!

Like golden apples in silver settings, so is a word spoken at the right time. ~ Proverbs 25:11 (GW)

When you pray, don't ramble like heathens who think they'll be heard if they talk a lot. ~ Matthew 6:7 (GW)

Church filled up on the first Sunday of the new year and as we listened to the organ prelude, my husband and I opened our hymnbooks to *The First Nowell*. John tapped my arm and pointed to a footnote on the page.

> "Note: In this carol, Nowell (Latin novella) means 'news,' and Noel (Latin natalis) means 'birthday.'"

Soon the congregation stood and we all sang: "The First Nowell [news] the angels did say…" And when we reached the refrain, we sang: "Noel, Noel, Noel, Noel [birthday] born is the King of Israel."

"How," I whispered to John, "could I have sung this carol all my life and not known this explanation until today?" "I don't know," he whispered back, "but I didn't know either." Two dunderheads!

I don't chastise myself for not knowing the meaning of these two Latin words; I chastise myself for singing them year after year without finding out what they mean. What other beliefs do I profess, but not truly understand?

So, this first Sunday of the new year, I made a resolution: I will not simply parrot the words of others. I treasure the beautiful, poetic words of the early hymns, but I'll learn the meaning of the words and the scriptural basis for them.

Prayer: Lord, when I sing your praises, when I share my faith with others, when I come to you in prayer, help me to use words I understand and feel in my heart. I don't want to simply copy others who sound wise or pious. I know, Lord, that you delight to welcome with warm embrace, those who are humble and sincere. Amen

Get to the Point[lxxvii]

I had studied hard. I knew the material well. So I felt mystified when my essay exam in Sociology came back with a poor grade. Feeling so thoroughly wronged, I did what I normally would be too timid to do. I paid a visit to my professor in his office to protest.

I believe I convinced this gracious man that I really did know the material. All the same, he insisted that I'd written around the answers instead of getting them committed to paper.

We reviewed my essays together, one after the other, and I had to admit he was right. If the exam had been two hours longer, perhaps I might have gotten to the point.

He upped my grade a bit, simply because I had come to speak with him. But as I left his office he said, "Just remember this: If you put enough monkeys at enough typewriters, eventually one of them will write the complete works of Shakespeare."

I did remember, and I did learn my lesson. Today when I write, I narrow my focus, and strive to hit that proverbial nail on the head.

Prayer: Lord, give me the words I need to share nuggets of truth.

~

Let thy speech be short, comprehending much in a few words.
~ Apocrypha

Jump Right In[lxxviii]

Day 1 of the school year always meant writing an essay entitled "My Summer Vacation" – an assignment I thoroughly enjoyed. I loved describing the mountains, the lake, swimming to a float anchored a little offshore. I wrote with ease about toasting marshmallows in the evening, snuggled with my sisters around a crackling campfire.

It is not so curious then, that my first publishing success as an adult was a similar piece. After vacationing in the Baltic, on the Swedish island of Gotland, I wrote up my travels. Then, without much forethought, I sent my nice little piece off to *Nordstjernan-Svea*, a New York-based Swedish weekly.

I acted on impulse, sending my English composition to a newspaper written largely in Swedish. To my delight, the editor published it, and requested two more articles! One subscriber commented, "I loved the piece on Gotland because I don't read Swedish. If you would publish more articles like this, I could read more of the paper." What fun is that!

Today I check the markets carefully before I submit my work; I seldom act on impulse. Yet, that one time I did. I broke with convention just a bit and success took me by surprise.

Prayer: Lord, enrich me with youthful verve.

~

It is only by following your deepest instinct that you can lead a rich life, and if you let your fear of consequence prevent you from following your deepest instinct, then your life will be safe, expedient and thin.
 – Katharine Butler Hathaway (1890-1942)

Nobody's Perfect[lxxix]

I came out of church feeling angry with myself. A friend sensed my agitation right away.

"What's wrong?" she asked.

I told her that I gave in, once again, to a serious character flaw; I let myself be distracted by poor grammar. She didn't get it.

"Well, I'll tell you," I confided. "When Pastor made the statement, 'God gives good gifts to you and I,' I lost it. I tuned out the rest of his sermon! Why must I always be persnickety? I'm such a judgmental person."

"Not at all," she assured me as we walked along together. Even though Adele was a fashion designer with talents very different from my own, she said she understood completely. "It's part of your job as a writer to be alert for such errors," she said. Then she added, "I stop listening to the sermon if the man seated in front of me is wearing a sports jacket and the plaid doesn't match at the back seam."

We laughed. Her sharing this about herself, helped put things in perspective for me. Now, whenever I hear "me" when it should be "I," or "I" when it should be "me," – or even the word "myself" when a simple "I" or "me" would be correct – I tell myself, "Oops, another mismatched seam" and I continue listening.

Prayer: Forgiving Father, help me to remember that I, too, make mistakes.

~

You and I do not see things as they are. We see things as we are.
– Henry Ward Beecher

Genevieve's Journal[lxxx]
(Essay)

Genevieve Cole lived in a world of parasols, petticoats, and "Prince Alberts," of biplanes and airdromes, of taffy pulls and headache powders. She was my husband's grandmother and back in 1911, when she was 17, she began keeping a diary.

I wish I had seen her diaries at a younger age, for reading them has taught me some valuable lessons. I had never before read another person's journal but it has influenced me so, that I now keep one myself.

I purchased a book of blank pages, the kind found near the cashier in every bookstore. You know the kind. They always sport the most attractive and romantic covers, ones that silently intimate the blank pages, when covered with script, will contain only the most precious gems of wisdom, insight and romance. Intimidated, I'd never bought one before. So what did I learn from Genevieve that gave me the courage?

The first thing I learned was to jot down the mundane even if it seems boring. Everybody's life is boring – in day-to-day "sound bites." I can't tell you how many days in 1911 "Gen" started her entry with "Did my ironing," or "Worked hard all day ironing," or "Came home early and ironed in the afternoon." Such tedious occupation. She ironed almost every day, yet she didn't think it too dull to mention. Her entries, only 3 or 4 sentences for each day, were crisp and to the point, so I kept reading. Then I found an entry that really surprised me. She wrote: "Tried ironing with carbon iron but gave it up."

Suddenly all the preceding pages jumped to life. The poor girl had been pushing the weighty irons that first needed to be heated on a wood-burning stove. No wonder it took so much of her time. How significant the insignificant now became and I gained real insight into the difficulties of housework before we had drip-dry fabrics. My respect for one young woman's diligence and hard work skyrocketed. How I admired her for all her other activities and intellectual pursuits in spite of the rigors of her life before electricity.

I'm so glad Genevieve didn't think the daily grind too insignificant to record. Now I'm doing the same. Who knows when society will advance to new ways and make my TV, computer, and automatic dishwasher obsolete – curious oddities for some future generation to ponder.

The second thing I learned is that I don't have to be noble on every page. I can and should record foibles, fears, and frustrations.

When Miss Cole began her "cadet" teaching assignment she recorded "Whatever made me think I wanted to be a teacher?" and "Had to whip a boy today for stealing," and "I'm just never going to be a teacher." But one day she also wrote, "Last day of school. Took picture of class. How I'll miss them."

She also wrote about refusing to date her roommate's boyfriend and how persistent he was anyway. I'm glad she recorded their first date and the jealous tirades she endured back at the dorm, because this is the man she married – my husband's grandfather – and I'm sure she didn't realize what the future held the first time she wrote his name in her book.

Finally, I'm glad she wrote about church and Sunday school even though it was the same week after week. She seldom missed a Sunday and that speaks of what was important to her. She often gave the sermon title or text. Sometimes she quoted Bible verses that spoke to her personally. Broad strokes but how they reveal her character!

Yes, Genevieve recorded only a few words each day but brevity is no doubt what kept her faithful! The daily entries convey very little when viewed singly. They speak volumes when considered as a whole – a virtual treasure chest of her daily activities, her fun-loving personality, and her strong faith in God. My hope, as I keep my diary, is to do likewise.

Yet, Not Yet, and You Bet!
(Speech at Toastmasters' Club)

Good afternoon fellow Toastmasters and honored guests.

Today I'd like to speak about the power of little words. Sometimes I think it's the little words that pack the most punch. Let me tell you three personal experiences with short words to prove my point.

When I was in college I met a campus chaplain with whom I had many interesting discussions. Then about 20 years later I met him again when I moved into a new community. I was so surprised to see him and I guess he, me. He asked what I'd been doing during all those intervening years and I told him how I'd completed a number of academic degrees in a couple of different colleges. Then I told him about my career in the business world and the various positions I'd held. Finally I told him about the guy I was about to marry.

"Sounds like you've had a wonderful life," he said. "Sounds like you've reached all your goals."

"No," I said, "not really. I always wanted to study communication and become a writer." Then rather wistfully I added, "I didn't do that." And he jumped in to add a word to complete my sentence: "yet."

What a powerful little word he spoke to me that day. He rekindled my interest. He resurrected a dormant dream. He gave me hope and encouragement with that simple three-letter word "yet."

I went to the library the next day. Researched the graduate schools within an hour's drive of my home and applied for admission. Twice a week for the next few years, I drove to class after commuting home from my job in Manhattan and completed a master's degree in communication. A long-time dream accomplished because someone was kind enough to say "yet."

Now let me tell you about "not yet." Last summer my 10-year old nephew flew in from San Jose to spend a week with my husband and me. We hadn't seen him in a few years and we had a delightful visit. Andrew is a beginner bagpipe student and he brought his practice chanter to show us. He also brought along a CD of his bagpipe teacher playing all sorts of jigs and reels.

Andrew stayed with us at our summer place on a lake in the Adirondacks and on Friday evening we took him to a concert at a nearby Christian camp. The stage was filled with high school and college musicians and they were terrific! They could play classical numbers, John Phillip Sousa marches, ragtime, rock, you name it. They were versatile.

After the program I suggested to Andrew that someday he too might play with a band. He seemed incredulous. He, comparing himself to the performers on stage said, "They're good. I can only play *Hot Cross Buns*."

This was now my chance to pass along the wisdom and encouragement I'd gotten from the campus chaplain. "Andrew," I said, "not yet. You cannot *yet* play as well, but you will one day if you keep practicing."

I told him that not that long ago, every single one of the students on stage that evening, could also "only play *Hot Cross Buns*." He looked surprised, almost as if he couldn't believe it. So I told him again. "Every single musician on that stage started with *Hot Cross Buns*. They are no different than you."

And now for the "you bet" story. A couple of months ago I went upstairs to see what my husband was doing. He'd been upstairs a long time and I was curious about what could be holding his interest for so long.

"What's so interesting?" I asked as I came up behind him and spied what he had on the computer screen. Guess what I saw! Cellos, lots of pictures of – would you believe it – cellos!

My hubby played the clarinet in high school and college on the West Coast. As a matter of fact he likes to brag about playing with the Oregon State University marching band in a *Rose Bowl Parade*. I never heard as much as a single toot from him on his clarinet. Now, here he was studying everything the Internet could provide about cellos.

"I want to learn how to play the cello," he said. "Think I can do that?" he asked and I responded, "You bet."

The next day he telephoned the local music school, rented an instrument and soon began taking lessons. Now every evening I hear him practice, beginning with – you guessed it – *Hot Cross Buns*.

"Yet," "Not yet," "You bet," – simple three-letter words. Can't get much smaller than that, but oh how powerful, how affirming, how motivating, how loving.

Friends, I'd like to encourage you in the same way. Whatever your hopes, your dreams, your aspirations, do I think you can do it? You bet!

About the Author

HELENE C. KUONI, a native New Yorker, graduated from Concordia Collegiate Institute (Bronxville, NY) and Hunter College (City University of New York). She holds a Master of Business Administration from Iona College (New Rochelle, NY) and a Master of Arts in Communication from Fairfield University (Fairfield, CT).

Helene is retired from employment in the oil industry, a short ESL (English as a Second Language) teaching assignment in the NYC public school system, staff positions in the house-counsel office of a major insurance firm, and an associate editor position with a Christian publishing house.

Helene's writing has been published in numerous devotional magazines, newspapers, and book compilations. She has also mentored new writers, that they might contribute to Advent Devotional Guides she compiled at two churches where the Kuonis were members. Today, she and her husband John reside in the Lehigh Valley, and are active members of *Grace Church Bethlehem* in Bethlehem, PA.

Helene pools the many skills garnered from her diverse career, with those of John. In addition to five books published with John, *A Walk in the Sunshine* is Helene's second book.

Production

JOHN P. KUONI grew up in Oregon and earned degrees in computer science from Oregon State University. He is now retired from a successful career in software development at various locations in Metropolitan New York.

A favorite retirement activity is researching his family tree and early American roots. John is descended from James Cole of Cole's Hill in Plymouth, Massachusetts (c. 1634), William Mead of Stamford, Connecticut (1635), and Francis Cooke who arrived on the Mayflower (1620).

After publishing a number of books concerning his family's forebears, John contributed his experience to the layout, formatting, and proof-reading tasks behind *A Walk in the Sunshine*. Helene reports that his support and help have been invaluable. She is most grateful, not only for his generous gift of time, advice, and assistance, but for suggesting this compilation and getting the whole project started.

References

Endnotes

[i] *The Secret Place, Devotions for Daily Worship.* Spring 2005. Judson Press, King of Prussia, Pennsylvania

[ii] *The Secret Place, Devotions for Daily Worship.* Spring 2007. Judson Press, King of Prussia, Pennsylvania

[iii] *Penned from the Heart (Volume 9)*, Son-Rise Publications, New Castle, Pennsylvania, 2002

[iv] *Penned from the Heart (Volume 9)*, Son-Rise Publications, New Castle, Pennsylvania, 2002

[v] *The Secret Place, Devotions for Daily Worship.* Spring 2003. Judson Press, King of Prussia, Pennsylvania

Penned from the Heart (Volume 20), Son-Rise Publications, New Castle, Pennsylvania, 2014

[vi] *The Secret Place, Devotions for Daily Worship.* Fall 2018. Judson Press, King of Prussia, Pennsylvania

[vii] *Penned from the Heart (Volume 21)*, Son-Rise Publications, New Castle, Pennsylvania, 2014

[viii] Similar version, *Advent Devotional Guide 2006*, Liberty Corner Presbyterian Church, Liberty Corner, New Jersey. Includes *Prayer: Loving Father, our celebration of Christ's birth with the beauty of glowing candles, the fragrance of balsam wreaths, the melodies of organ, strings and flute—warm us to your love, and stir memories of Christmases past in our hearts. Assure your children here on earth, that their loved ones with Christ sing hymns of praise this season and always. Amen*

[ix] *The Secret Place, Devotions for Daily Worship.* Spring 2003. Judson Press, King of Prussia, Pennsylvania

Penned from the Heart (Volume 20), Son-Rise Publications, New Castle, Pennsylvania, 2014

[x] Similar version: *The Secret Place, Devotions for Daily Worship.* Spring 2006. Judson Press, King of Prussia, Pennsylvania

[xi] *Penned from the Heart (Volume 6)*, Son-Rise Publications, New Castle, Pennsylvania, 1999

[xii] *Penned from the Heart (Volume 6)*, Son-Rise Publications, New Castle, Pennsylvania, 1999

[xiii] *Penned from the Heart (Volume 5)*, Son-Rise Publications, New Castle, Pennsylvania, 1998

[xiv] *RISE: 32 Weeks of Inspiring Devotions to Fuel Your First Year of College*, Chaplain Publishing, Lubbock, Texas, 2014

Similar version "Faith under Pressure" *The Secret Place, Devotions for Daily Worship.* Winter 2009-2010. Judson Press, King of Prussia, Pennsylvania. Includes *Prayer: Heavenly Father, kindest teacher of all, when life introduces difficult "music," may my faith hold secure, grow strong, and produce a symphony of praise; in Jesus' name. Amen*

[xv] *Advent Devotional Guide 1998*, Liberty Corner Presbyterian Church, Liberty Corner, New Jersey

Penned from the Heart (Volume 5), Son-Rise Publications, New Castle, Pennsylvania, 1998

Similar version *2012 Advent to Epiphany Devotional Guide*, Union Evangelical Lutheran Church, Schnecksville, Pennsylvania

[xvi] *The Secret Place, Devotions for Daily Worship.* Summer 1999. Judson Press, King of Prussia, Pennsylvania

Penned from the Heart (Volume VII), Son-Rise Publications, New Castle, Pennsylvania, 2000

An Hour of Power (Worship bulletin, Tues., Oct. 31, 2000), Clinton Memorial A.M.E. Zion Church, Newark, New Jersey

[xvii] *The Secret Place, Devotions for Daily Worship*. Spring 2005. Judson Press, King of Prussia, Pennsylvania

[xviii] *The Secret Place, Devotions for Daily Worship*. Summer 2001. Judson Press, King of Prussia, Pennsylvania

Penned from the Heart (Volume 9), Son-Rise Publications, New Castle, Pennsylvania, 2002

[xix] *Penned from the Heart (Volume 6)*, Son-Rise Publications, New Castle, Pennsylvania, 1999

[xx] *Lighthouse Story Collections: Timeless Stories and Poems for Family Reading*, Number 50. Watauga, Texas, April 2000

[xxi] *A Cup of Comfort Devotional for Women*, Edited by James Stuart Bell and Carol McLean Wilde, Adams Media, an F+W Publications Company, Avon, Massachusetts, 2005 [*salvation* rendered *peace*]

The Hollwegs Choir Journal, © 2011 Helene C. Kuoni, Allentown, Pennsylvania
Different Title: Epilogue
Modified as follows:
-      Second paragraph from end *"...--the memory of parents who kept Christ in Christmas."*
-      Last paragraph addition: *"For Thyra, Dorothy, Helene and Marilyn, "a loving family" most definitely includes our brothers and sisters in The Hollwegs Choir. How great the blessings that God bestows—the gift of music and the gift of others whose lives point to Christ and the path of salvation."*

Similar version, *2010 Advent to Epiphany Devotional Guide*, Union Evangelical Lutheran Church, Schnecksville, Pennsylvania. Included

Prayer: Heavenly Father, be with us as we decide what gifts we'll give to others this Christmas. And thank you for the greatest gift of all—your love to us in Jesus.

[xxii] *The Hollwegs Choir Journal*, © 2011 Helene C. Kuoni, Allentown, Pennsylvania

[xxiii] *The Hollwegs Choir Journal*, © 2011 Helene C. Kuoni, Allentown, Pennsylvania

[xxiv] *Memories of Mother: Inspiring REAL-LIFE STORIES of how MOTHERS touch OUR LIVES*. Xulon Press, a division of Salem Media Group, Maitland, Florida, 2007

[xxv] *Advent Devotional Guide 2001*, Liberty Corner Presbyterian Church, Liberty Corner, New Jersey

[xxvi] *2011 Advent to Epiphany Devotional Guide*, Union Evangelical Lutheran Church, Schnecksville, Pennsylvania

Similar version *Liberty Corner Presbyterian Church 2005 Advent Devotional*, Liberty Corner, New Jersey

[xxvii] *The Secret Place, Devotions for Daily Worship.* Summer 2004. Judson Press, King of Prussia, Pennsylvania

[xxviii] *Penned from the Heart (Volume 9)*, Son-Rise Publications, New Castle, Pennsylvania, 2002

[xxix] *2013 Advent to Epiphany Devotional Guide*, Union Evangelical Lutheran Church, Schnecksville, Pennsylvania

[xxx] *2014 Advent to Epiphany Devotional Guide*, Union Evangelical Lutheran Church, Schnecksville, Pennsylvania

[xxxi] *Advent Devotional Guide 1996*, Liberty Corner Presbyterian Church, Liberty Corner, New Jersey

Penned from the Heart (Volume IV), Son-Rise Publications, New Castle, Pennsylvania, 1997, without prayer

[xxxii] *GOD'S Little Rule Book, Simple Rules to Bring Joy and Happiness To Your Life.* Starburst Publishers, Lancaster, Pennsylvania. 1999

Penned from the Heart (Volume X), Entitled: Quit Praying! Son-Rise Publications, New Castle, Pennsylvania, 2003

[xxxiii] *We Support You! Letters of Encouragement for Our Troops Serving in Iraq and Afghanistan.* Xulon Press, a division of Salem Media Group, Maitland, Florida, 2008

[xxxiv] *Penned from the Heart (Volume 9),* Son-Rise Publications, New Castle, Pennsylvania, 2002

[xxxv] *Love is a Verb Devotional* by Gary Chapman with James Stuart Bell, Bethany House Publishers, Bloomington, Minnesota, 2011

[xxxvi] *Love is a Verb Devotional* by Gary Chapman with James Stuart Bell, Bethany House Publishers, Bloomington, Minnesota, 2011

[xxxvii] *Penned from the Heart (Volume 9),* Son-Rise Publications, New Castle, Pennsylvania, 2002

[xxxviii] *GOD STORIES from South Central Pennsylvania—Volume Eight.* The Regional Church of Lancaster County, Lancaster, Pennsylvania, 2012

[xxxix] *The Secret Place, Devotions for Daily Worship.* Summer 1999. Judson Press, King of Prussia, Pennsylvania

Penned from the Heart (Volume VII), Son-Rise Publications, New Castle, Pennsylvania, 2000

An Hour of Power (Worship bulletin, Tues., Oct. 17, 2000.), Clinton Memorial A.M.E. Zion Church, Newark, New Jersey

[xl] *Lenten Devotional Guide, Spring 2000,* Liberty Corner Presbyterian Church, Liberty Corner, New Jersey

Penned from the Heart (Volume VIII), Son-Rise Publications, New Castle, Pennsylvania, 2001, Prayer omits reference to *"this Lenten season."*

[xli] *Guia Devocional Para la Temporada de Navidad 2001, En Espanol y Ingles/Advent Devotional Guide.* Liberty Corner Presbyterian Church, Liberty Corner, New Jersey (Spanish paraphrase for mission church in Honduras. LCPC translator unknown.)

[xlii] *A Growing Heart—Stories, Lessons, and Exercises Inspired by PROVERBS,* Edited by Kathy Collard Miller, Starburst Publishers, Lancaster, Pennsylvania, Sept. 2001

[xliii] *Advent Devotional Guide 1997*, Liberty Corner Presbyterian Church, Liberty Corner, New Jersey

Penned from the Heart (Volume 5), Son-Rise Publications, New Castle, Pennsylvania, 1998

2011 Advent to Epiphany Devotional Guide, Union Evangelical Lutheran Church, Schnecksville, Pennsylvania. Includes *Prayer: Faithful Father, you keep your promises, and we can rely on your word. Help us to remain faithful, too.*

[xliv] *The Secret Place, Devotions for Daily Worship.* Spring 2003. Judson Press, King of Prussia, Pennsylvania

[xlv] *Penned from the Heart (Volume 5)*, Son-Rise Publications, New Castle, Pennsylvania, 1998

[xlvi] *A Cup of Comfort, Book of Prayer*, Edited by James Stuart Bell and Susan B. Townsend, Adams Media, an F+W Publications Company, Avon, Massachusetts, 2007

[xlvii] *The Secret Place, Devotions for Daily Worship.* Fall 2011. Judson Press, King of Prussia, Pennsylvania

[xlviii] *Penned from the Heart (Volume 6)*, Son-Rise Publications, New Castle, Pennsylvania, 1999

[xlix] *Treasures of a Woman's Heart, A Daybook of Stories and Inspiration*, Edited by Lynn D. Morrissey. Starburst Publishers, Lancaster, Pennsylvania, 2000

[l] *The Secret Place, Devotions for Daily Worship*. Spring 2007. Judson Press, King of Prussia, Pennsylvania

Unknown translator posted Chinese version on the Internet, Spring 2007.

2011 Advent to Epiphany Devotional Guide, Union Evangelical Lutheran Church, Schnecksville, Pennsylvania. Includes *Prayer: O Holy God, Creator and Judge of the universe, I recognize and confess my faults and failings. Today, in the middle of this Advent season, clothe me in the garments of salvation available only through your Son, Christ Jesus; in his name I pray. Amen*

[li] *Advent Devotional Guide 1999*, Liberty Corner Presbyterian Church, Liberty Corner, New Jersey

Penned from the Heart (Volume VIII), Son-Rise Publications, New Castle, Pennsylvania, 2001

[lii] *Penned from the Heart (Volume IV)*, Son-Rise Publications, New Castle, Pennsylvania, 1997

Similar version: *Advent Devotional Guide 1996*, Liberty Corner Presbyterian Church, Liberty Corner, New Jersey

[liii] *GOD'S Little Rule Book, Simple Rules to Bring Joy and Happiness To Your Life*, Starburst Publishers, Lancaster, Pennsylvania, 1999

Penned from the Heart (Volume X), entitled: Too Hot to Handle, Son-Rise Publications, New Castle, Pennsylvania, 2003

[liv] *GOD'S Little Rule Book, Simple Rules to Bring Joy and Happiness To Your Life*, Starburst Publishers, Lancaster, Pennsylvania. 1999

Penned from the Heart (Volume X), Entitled: Train-ing for Life. Son-Rise Publications, New Castle, Pennsylvania, 2003

lv *The Secret Place, Devotions for Daily Worship.* Summer 1999. Judson Press, King of Prussia, Pennsylvania

Penned from the Heart (Volume VII), Son-Rise Publications, New Castle, Pennsylvania, 2000

An Hour of Power (Worship bulletin, Tues., Oct. 23, 2000) Clinton Memorial A.M.E. Zion Church, Newark, New Jersey

lvi *The Secret Place, Devotions for Daily Worship.* Summer 1999. Judson Press, King of Prussia, Pennsylvania

Penned from the Heart (Volume VII), Son-Rise Publications, New Castle, Pennsylvania, 2000

Penned from the Heart (Volume X), Son-Rise Publications, New Castle, Pennsylvania, 2003

lvii *The Secret Place, Devotions for Daily Worship.* Winter 2001-2002 Judson Press, King of Prussia, Pennsylvania

Penned from the Heart (Volume X), Son-Rise Publications, New Castle, Pennsylvania, 2003

The Spiritual Voice News, Kennett Square, Pennsylvania, Spring 2005

lviii *Penned from the Heart (Volume VII)*, Son-Rise Publications, New Castle, Pennsylvania, 2000

lix *Penned from the Heart (Volume VIII)*, Son-Rise Publications, New Castle, Pennsylvania, 2001

lx *Penned from the Heart (Volume 9)*, Son-Rise Publications, New Castle, Pennsylvania, 2002

lxi *Daily Guideposts 2003*, Guideposts, Carmel, New York, 2002

lxii *Nordstjernan-Svea*, New York, New York, September 6, 1984 [lxiii] *Nordstjernan-Svea*, New York, New York, September 20, 1984

[lxiv] *Nordstjernan-Svea*, New York, New York, February 21, 1985

[lxv] *Nordstjernan-Svea*, New York, New York, February 20, 1986

Norden (Reprint), Brooklyn, New York, February 26, 1986

[lxvi] *The Hollwegs Choir Journal*, © 2011 Helene C. Kuoni, Allentown, Pennsylvania

[lxvii] *Treasures of a Woman's Heart, A Daybook of Stories and Inspiration*, Edited by Lynn D. Morrissey. Starburst Publishers, Lancaster, Pennsylvania, 2000

[lxviii] *GOD'S Little Rule Book, Simple Rules to Bring Joy and Happiness To Your Life*, Starburst Publishers, Lancaster, Pennsylvania, 1999

Penned from the Heart (Volume X), Entitled: Two Virtues for the Heart. Son-Rise Publications, New Castle, Pennsylvania, 2003

[lxix] *Treasures of a Woman's Heart, A Daybook of Stories and Inspiration*, Edited by Lynn D. Morrissey. Starburst Publishers, Lancaster, Pennsylvania, 2000

[lxx] *GOD'S Little Rule Book, Simple Rules to Bring Joy and Happiness To Your Life*, Starburst Publishers, Lancaster, Pennsylvania, 1999

[lxxi] *The Secret Place, Devotions for Daily Worship.* Summer 2000. Judson Press, King of Prussia, Pennsylvania

Penned from the Heart (Volume VIII), Son-Rise Publications, New Castle, Pennsylvania, 2001

But Drops of Grief .... Can Ne'er Repay (1999 Lenten Booklet) Clinton Memorial A.M.E. Zion Church, Newark, New Jersey

[lxxii] *RISE: 32 Weeks of Inspiring Devotions to Fuel Your First Year of College*, Chaplain Publishing, Lubbock, Texas, 2014

Similar version, *The Secret Place, Devotions for Daily Worship.* Spring 2006. Judson Press, King of Prussia, Pennsylvania

Similar version, *Liberty Corner Presbyterian Church 2004 Advent Devotional*, Liberty Corner, New Jersey

[lxxiii] *GOD'S Little Rule Book, Simple Rules to Bring Joy and Happiness To Your Life*, Starburst Publishers, Lancaster, Pennsylvania. 1999

Penned from the Heart (Volume X), Entitled: The Well-fought Fight. Son-Rise Publications, New Castle, Pennsylvania, 2003

[lxxiv] *LIFE'S Little Rule Book, Simple Rules to Bring Joy and Happiness To Your Life*, Starburst Publishers, Lancaster, Pennsylvania, 1999

[lxxv] *Penned from the Heart (Volume 9)*, Son-Rise Publications, New Castle, Pennsylvania, 2002

[lxxvi] *"A Perfect Relationship: You and God"* (2000 Lenten Booklet) Clinton Memorial A.M.E. Zion Church, Newark, New Jersey, 2000

[lxxvii] *Daily Devotions for Writers, from The Writing Academy,* Compiled and edited by Patricia Lorenz, West Conshohocken, Pennsylvania, March 2008

[lxxviii] *Daily Devotions for Writers, from The Writing Academy,* Compiled and edited by Patricia Lorenz, West Conshohocken, Pennsylvania, March 2008

[lxxix] *Daily Devotions for Writers, from The Writing Academy,* Compiled and edited by Patricia Lorenz, West Conshohocken, Pennsylvania, March 2008

[lxxx] *The Diaries of Genevieve Cole: 1911, 1913-1917 (Second Edition)* © 1999, 2018 by John P. Kuoni, Allentown, Pennsylvania

Photographs

<u>Page</u>   <u>Description</u>

Cover
- *Granite Fountain (1871), City Hall Park, New York, NY (2007)*

Section page: Solid Ground of God's Word
- *View of the Hudson River from Boscobel Historic House and Gardens, Garrison, NY (2004)*

Whose Leaf Does not Wither
- *Aunt Lilly on 90th birthday, Manchester, NJ (July 9, 2001)*

Section page: Fair Days of Fellowship and Church
- *Helene at Redeemer Lutheran Church, Elliott Ave., Yonkers, NY (1963)*

Old-Fashioned Coffee Time
- *Helene in her Mobil Oil Corporation office overlooking 42nd St., NYC (1989)*
- *"Nana" (Helene's maternal grandmother) (c. 1950)*

Dorothy's All-Time Favorite Carol
- *Dorothy at organ console, First Reformed Church, Hastings-on-Hudson, NY (early 1970s)*

Section page: Sunrise of New Beginnings
- *Throgs Neck Bridge (connects the Bronx and Queens, NY); East River meets Long Island Sound (2009)*

Section page: Sun, Moon, and Stars – God's Faithfulness in Nature
- *Lake Pleasant (in Adirondack Park), NY in winter (2008)*

Beauty Secrets
- *Wildflowers, Grand Teton National Park, WY (1979)*

Hold Fast to Your Faith
- *With family and musician friends at Lake Pleasant, NY (2009)*

Keeping the Faith
- *NYPD chaplain Rev. William Gillies Kalaidjian (1989)*

Section page: Fog of Fear and Indecision
- *Day trip with Judy and her sister Ruth Ann, Connecticut (1980)*

Me—At Age Three
- *Goeckeler Bakery window, Woodlawn Heights (Bronx), NY (c. 1948)*

Section page: Refreshing Times of Friendship
- *Thyra's birthday (5th from left); Dorothy and Helene to Thyra's right, and Woodlawn friends (c. 1947)*

A Heart Made Fit for Friendship
- *Judy and Helene ice skating, lake on Bronx River Parkway, Scarsdale, NY (c. 1958). Photo by Herbert Lischke*

Christmas 2008
- *Record snowfall, Lake Pleasant, NY (2008)*
- *Friends Laurie, Leslie, Steve, Marietta at Lake Pleasant (2008)*
- *Helene and John in Phillies attire, Allentown, PA (2008)*

Section page: Billowing Clouds of Witness
- *Estes Park, CO (1979)*

Tracks in the Snow
- *John, Basking Ridge, NJ (2000)*

Section page: Waterfalls of God's Love
- *Silver Falls State Park, Silverton, OR (1996)*

To Curry Favor
- *Thyra, Helene, Dorothy, and Marilyn Hollwegs with opera star Werner Hollweg, Salzburg, Austria (1983)*

Section page: Morningstar, Direction of the Family
- *Family portrait at Grandma's (father's mother), Woodllawn Heights (early 1950s)*

My Dad's Christmas
- *Christmas morning, Woodlawn Heights (1950s)*

Mom
- *Helen Hollwegs (Mom), Bronxville, NY (c. 1971)*
- *Helen Hollwegs (Mom) with Dorothy (1940s)*

Dad
- *Fred. H. Hollwegs (Dad) NYPD Band*

Drummer Dad
- *"Fred the Cop" at old entrance gates to the New York Bronx Zoo*

Clothed in Her Love
- *Helene in her mother's arms*

Section page: Dawn of the Holy Spirit
- *Winter sunrise over Lake Pleasant, NY (2005)*

Bread of Life
- *Mural on side of building, Chillicothe, MO (2014)*

Section page: Orbits of Kingdom Work
- *John with nephew Andrew, Lake Pleasant, NY (2003)*

Good Gossip
- *John with Marie of "Donuts and More," Speculator, NY (2003)*

Section page: Threatening Storm Clouds of Difficulty
- *Lake Pleasant, NY (2007)*

The Puffback
- *Helene and John, Clinton, NJ (1994)*

Flames of Prayer
- *Lake Pleasant, NY campfire (2008)*

Section page: God's Promises and Power in Creation
- *Hummingbird feeder, Adirondack Museum, Blue Mountain Lake, NY (2008)*

The Sky-High Promise
- *Rainbow over Lake Pleasant, NY (2008)*

Uphill Battles and Bountiful Blessings
- *Nature Walk, Speculator, NY (2004)*

Section page: Sunset Rest
- *Villas of Trexler Park, Allentown, PA (2009)*

Scripture page: Matthew 11:28-30 (NIV)
- *Mittenwald (Bavaria), Germany (1983)*

Relax
- *John at Lake Pleasant, NY (2007)*

Section page: Harvest of Salvation
- *Along New York Route 23 in the vicinity of Catskill-Cairo (2002)*

Section page: Storms of Temptation
- *E. 237 St., Woodlawn Heights, aftermath of hurricane (Sept. 1944)*

Preparing for Snakes
- *Black bears, Route 8, Lake Pleasant, NY (2007)*

Section page: Nighttime of Trust and Peace
- *Bavaria, Germany (1983)*

Deep Waters
- *Karen and Helene touring Statue of Liberty, NY Harbor (c. 1990)*

Sure Steps
- *Lake Pleasant, NY (2007)*

Relinquishing My Will
- *Dad, Dorothy, and Helene (on bike), E. 237th St., Woodlawn Heights (early 1950s)*

Section page: Clear Skies of Thankfulness
- *Lake Pleasant, NY (2008)*

Daily Guideposts Reader's Room: A Helping Hand
- *Helene (2003)*

Section page: Trails to Travel
- *Helene and John, Westfield, MA (2004)*

Gotland—Top and Center
- *Visby, Gotland, Sweden (1984)*
- *Martebo, Gotland, Sweden (1984)*
- *Martebo Church, Gotland, Sweden (1984)*

Dalarna First
- *Tällberg (Dalarna), Sweden (1984)*
- *Dala horse factory, Village of Nusnäs (Dalarna), Sweden (1984)*

Cruising the Göta Canal
- *Helene and tour guide (also named Helene) on Göta Canal, Sweden (1984)*
- *Karlsborg, Sweden (1984)*

NORDLEK '85 with Swedish Folk Dancers
- *Swedish Folk Dancers of New York at Christina Park, Wilmington, DE (1985)*
- *Gotland folk costumes, ScanFest, Budd Lake, NJ (1985)*

Section page: Dewdrops of Wisdom
- *Butterflies on Goldenrod, Speculator, NY (2001)*

Dorothy
- *Dorothy (1960)*
- *On grounds of Texaco Corporate Headquarters, Harrison, NY (1977)*
- *Dorothy, organist at Hollwegs Choir event, Greenville Community Reformed Church - Scarsdale, NY (1986)*

Section page: Gardens of Grace
- *Villas of Trexler Park, Allentown, PA (2010)*

Miss Lungen's Legacy
- *Dorothy Lungen at 88 years of age, Bronx, NY (1983)*
- *Dorothy Lungen (1983)*

Section page: Moonglow of Childhood Memories
- *(L to R) Dorothy, Thyra, Helene picking apples*
- *Sandbox with second cousin Johnny Boy, Bronx, NY (c. 1946)*
- *Woodlawn Heights June Walk - Thyra holding Helene's hand (early 1950s)*
- *336 E. 236 St., Woodlawn, July 4th*
- *336 E. 236 St., Woodlawn, after a snowstorm*
- *Christmas at 336 E. 236th St., Woodlawn (c. 1948)*
- *St. Mark's Sunday school outing, Hudson River Day Line steamer,* Alexander Hamilton *(1950s)*
- *Circle Line Boat Ride around Manhattan Island (early 1950s)*
- *Helene with P.S. 19, Bronx classmates (c. 1954)*

Section page: The Wellspring of Wisdom
- *Woodstock (Catskill Mountains), NY*

Yet, Not Yet, and You Bet!
- *Nephew Andrew, Lake Pleasant, NY (2004)*

Sources

Essay/Article	Source
Keeping the Faith	Interviews with and files of Rev. William G. Kalaidjian
Drummer Dad	*New York Daily News* news article, c. 1930s
NORKLEK '85	Travel notes of Richard Haggblad (Swedish Folk Dancers of NY)
Saint Patrick's Day Parade	*New York Times* news articles: March 1935, '39, '41, '43, '44, '53

www.ingramcontent.com/pod-product-compliance
Lightning Source LLC
Chambersburg PA
CBHW062021290426
44108CB00024B/2731